First published in 2008
© Demos. Some rights reserved
Magdalen House, 136 Tooley Street,
London, SE1 2TU, UK

ISBN 978 1 84180 200 8
Copy edited by Julie Pickard, London
Series design by modernactivity
Typeset by Chat Noir Design, Charente
Printed by Lecturis, Eindhoven

Set in Gotham Rounded
and Baskerville 10
Cover paper: Flora Gardenia
Text paper: Munken Premium White

THE FUTURE FACE OF ENTERPRISE

Edited by Shawnee Keck
and Alessandra Buonfino

COLLECTION 26

DEM☉S

Contents

Acknowledgements

We would like to thank the Make Your Mark campaign run by Enterprise Insight for their generous support of this collection and we are enormously grateful to all those who contributed essays and viewpoints, and those whose comments and feedback have helped to shape it: Charlie Edwards, Catherine Fieschi, Milly Getachew, Peter Harrington, William Higham, Simon Parker, Amin Samman and Molly Webb.

Shawnee Keck
Alessandra Buonfino
July 2008

Foreword

Raj Patel

We all aspire to better standards of living and we depend on growth and productivity to deliver this. Nothing more than enterprise signifies a nation's confidence and the desire to strive for improvement to better itself. For the Make Your Mark Campaign, people making their ideas happen is the core essence of enterprise, and creating enterprising places, spaces and mindsets is at the heart of that challenge.

When it comes to making economies more dynamic and innovative, Edmund Phelps, the renowned economist and winner of the 2006 Nobel Prize in Economics, finds it surprising that so much time is spent on economic institutions when attitudes towards risk-taking, responsibility and team-working actually do a significantly better job at explaining performance differences between countries than institutional factors. From another part of the world, Dr Abdul Kalam, the renowned scientist, former President of India and not a stranger to hardship and dreaming big, proclaimed that his single mission was to meet and 'ignite' at least 100,000 students to shape a new India.

Each generation defines enterprise according to its own needs and priorities. Indeed, contrary to popular perceptions, our notion of entrepreneurs and their role in society has not been static over the decades but continues to evolve. In reinventing a Britain that is fit for the twenty-first century we need to reassess the challenges we face and pursue a constant drive to find new ideas and new ways of stimulating enterprise to meet today's needs, challenges and opportunities.

So as we look ahead to helping to deliver the ambitions of the recently published Enterprise Strategy[1] is the challenge we face simply about encouraging more enterprise or is it also about creating a different kind of enterprise? What is the future face of enterprise? For some this is simply about the economy. Yet for others, like Professor Raymond Kao, author of *Entrepreneurism: A philosophy and a sensible alternative for the market economy*, enterprise should not be viewed just as a means for wealth creation, but also as something that can contribute to the common good.

This collection of essays aims to inform the debate about the future face of enterprise. It contains a wide range of opinions by renowned authors with expertise in their field, entrepreneurs, educationalists and business leaders. It does not attempt to predict the future. Neither is it a comprehensive stocktaking of enterprise culture, for trying to cover the broad agenda of enterprise in a single publication would be impossible. It serves to illuminate possibilities and perspectives on shaping the future of an enterprising UK. It is also timely, as enterprise and innovation is placed at the heart of a range of new developments in education, business support and economic regeneration.

We are grateful to all those who have contributed their ideas and to Demos in helping to pull together such diverse topics and views. Building an enterprise culture depends on exploiting new possibilities and there are hundreds of things that have to change – from what's in our text books to how society incentivises risk-taking. If you have insights or ideas about the future face of enterprise, please do take the opportunity to contribute through the campaign website – www.makeyourmark.org.uk/policy. I hope that the ideas emerging from this series of essays will encourage, inform and challenge you to consider how to bring to life a face of enterprise that is fit for the future.

Raj Patel, is Director of Policy, Make Your Mark campaign.

Make Your Mark is the national campaign to unlock the UK's enterprise potential. The campaign, run by Enterprise Insight, was founded by the British Chambers of Commerce, the CBI, the Federation of Small Businesses and the Institute of Directors. It is supported by the Department for Business, Enterprise and Regulatory Reform.

Introduction

Our aim is to widen and deepen the enterprise culture in our country so that every woman and every man – regardless of background or circumstance – has the chance to go as far as their talents and potential will take them, so that enterprise is truly open to all.
   Gordon Brown, 2002[1]

   It is just before their summer holidays and the 15-year-old students at Didcot Girls School in Oxfordshire are anxious to get out of class, but they sit patiently to answer some questions: 'What is an entrepreneur, can anyone name someone they know? What are the characteristics of an entrepreneur? Would you want to start your own business? What type of business would you start? How much does starting a business cost?' We will return to the Didcot girls for some answers, but first let's take a look at some of the wider context around the way we understand and promote enterprise.

   Demos has been tracking the evolution of this particular field for more than ten years. In 1996, Geoff Mulgan and Perri 6 heralded 'the new enterprise culture', evoking the possibility of a second renaissance during which the detached entrepreneur operating as an outsider was replaced by an understanding of entrepreneurship rooted in networks, collaborative working and partnerships – all in the context of a new information economy. Writing in the mid 1990s, they argued that the new enterprise culture would depend more on networks and partnerships than on the success of lone individuals; that new organisational forms that valued continued learning would be required to assist the move from the industrial economy to one based on information and services; and that space would have to be made for employee input and imagination in order to shape the future workplace. They also saw government's role as facilitating this culture rather than merely regulating it. The new culture would promote 'a truly healthy and adaptive economy where everyone can imagine themselves as an entrepreneur, owning their own life, and where everyone can imagine taking a small slice of their savings or pension capital to invest in a friend or relative's business'.[2]

A decade later, in 2004, the Make Your Mark campaign – run by Enterprise Insight, founded by the four main business organisations and funded by the then-Department for Trade and Industry (DTI)[3] – was created to help develop such an enterprise culture and do this by inspiring young people to turn their business dreams into reality. The coalition they established included businesses, education, enterprise development organisations and government. It defined enterprise simply as 'having an idea and making it happen' and entrepreneurship as 'new venture creation and development'. The campaign argued that discovering new ways of doing things would require not just structural change but behavioural change on the part of individuals – both in terms of a self-belief in taking managed risks as well as in being creative.

The campaign also highlighted the need for a more supportive society to make this happen and to encourage and reward these actions. They advocated the now widely accepted idea that enterprise needed to be integral not only to business and government but also to education (in schools, colleges and universities). Education in particular has a critical role to play in developing 'enterprise capability' among young people, described by the Department for Children, Schools and Families (DCSF) as creativity, innovation, risk-management and risk-taking, a 'can-do' attitude and the drive to make ideas happen. Here, investment has led to massive strides being made particularly for 14–16-year-olds at Key Stage 4 of the National Curriculum.

Which brings us back to Didcot Girls School. How well is enterprise policy meeting its goal through this group? Is enterprise evident in the way they see the world, their career aspirations or their plans for the summer break? Well, not quite yet, but they do say that enterprise education has made them aware of future opportunities. They knew what entrepreneurship meant and could even name a few entrepreneurs, such as Anita Roddick, an auntie who owned a spa, and 'the Google guys'. None of them wanted to start their own business right away, but many were interested in doing so after university. They talked of business start-ups and suspected it would take at least £250,000 to get a business off the ground.[4]

The girls' answers suggest some progress but they also point to some of the remaining challenges in advancing the enterprise agenda. Entrepreneurship might seem a more acceptable and understood option for many, but a challenge still remains in identifying the strategies that will instil a sustainable, lasting cultural change.

Leading change in enterprise policy

Part of the issue with concepts like 'entrepreneurship' or 'enterprise' is that they are multidimensional and multi-disciplinary. Contrary to some people's views, enterprise is not just a business topic; it comprises economics, politics, psychology, sociology, geography and management.[5]

Change is more difficult to pinpoint: cultural and multidisciplinary objectives by their nature are difficult to define and analyse, have delayed outcomes, and are always extremely contextual.[6] Making policy for these areas is also difficult since the triggers and levers of influence are always uncertain. It is not a question of creating an initiative one day and expecting a host of new, strong, business start-ups the next. Not only would this objective be based on a ludicrously narrow definition of what 'enterprise' is – it would also be based on a simplistic understanding of the relationship between business start-ups and the contribution to sustainable economic development. Programmes that work in one location may fall flat in another; even in an age of globalisation, economies are often very rooted in their more immediate local area. Essentially, policy is faced with stewarding something that is hard to pinpoint.

On top of definitional complexity, embedding an enterprise culture in the everyday lives of children and adults can feel like an overwhelming task. A new culture requires building a new social movement. Changing a culture is, essentially, a generational process that requires patience and a cathedral builder's mentality. The stones put in place today are just a start. This society will not see the finished building; all we can do is ensure that we leave strong foundations in order that the next generation fulfils its own potential.

What progress?

Enterprise is important primarily because of its potential as a force for economic development – also recognised by the Treasury as one of five drivers of productivity. The UK was able to halt the trend of small business decline that occurred between 1910 and 1960; by 1990, rates were back up to the level of 1910[7] and the small firm was back. Today, multiple studies have demonstrated that, in general, new firm start-ups, self-employment and a vibrant small business sector have a strong influence on GDP growth.[8]

Small firms currently employ 58 per cent of the private sector workforce contributing over 50 per cent of GDP. They account for more than 99 per cent of all UK businesses, and in 2006 they generated £2,600 billion, up by 6.8 per cent from 2005.[9] Although most of the Organisation for Economic Co-operation and Development (OECD) countries have seen a decline in entrepreneurial activity, the UK has managed to maintain its own levels relatively steady since 1997.[10] The World Bank ranks the UK second in Europe, and sixth out of 178 economies on measures of the ease of doing business. The UK also has the third highest business survival rate in the OECD, which means start-up activity is producing sustainable businesses.[11]

But are British people any more enterprising today than in the past? Developing an enterprise culture is a process of fits and starts and it is difficult to determine policy effects on short-term analysis. Yet, there are cultural signs: more people are trading on eBay, and TV programmes like *Dragon's Den* and *The Apprentice* are extremely popular. In 2006, 7.8 per cent of people polled said they would expect to start a new business in the next three years, up from 4.6 per cent in 2002; and Britain tops the OECD charts in terms of positive attitudes towards entrepreneurship.[12]

Enterprise is entering the aspirations of many people around the country too – both young and old. Over half of the EU's young people (15–24-year-olds) who were not currently self-employed stated that they would like to follow an entre-preneurial path compared with 42 per cent in the US. Not everyone may eventually decide to become an entrepreneur, but building up enterprise culture can nonetheless provide young people with new skills, opportunities and outlooks. As Martha Lane Fox argues in this collection, 'creating an enterprise culture... needs to start at home and at school'.

The geographical distribution of enterprise culture is also still patchy. While entrepreneurial energy is strong in some places, evidence suggests that enterprise has not permeated all realms of society, and that we are not all setting up businesses – there may be regional or local biases, there may be particular enterprise hubs and clusters around the country. By its nature, enterprise takes place in multiple sites and spaces and in varied forms. Enterprise is a bit of a chameleon – it adapts to its context and becomes part of the landscape thus making it integral to a particular place but often difficult to detect, track and measure.

It is also the domain of a number of public policy areas. It occupies a diverse space that ranges from schools and young people to community organisations and the financial sector. Yet its contribution and role are not yet fully recognised. For instance, a recent Department for Work and Pensions green paper doesn't mention enterprise as a way to get disadvantaged people back to work,[13] whereas developments in the Cabinet Office and the third sector are placing social enterprise at the forefront of new approaches.[14] The recent Department for Culture, Media and Sport culture strategy extols the virtues of turning creative talent into productive businesses, yet the recent Communities and Local Government consultation assessing indicators of performance for local government used a definition of enterprise that only took into account business start-ups.

Enterprise education seems to be at the heart of Business and Enterprise schools, but what about other specialisms? And how deeply embedded is enterprise in colleges and universities? To what extent are human resources directors of companies really looking for entrepreneurially minded people?

The future face of enterprise: where next?

The Treasury wants enterprise for all, and the Prime Minister has argued that there should be no 'no go' areas for enterprise. So, can this be achieved in the future? What is the next phase in the development of enterprise culture and what are the forces that are shaping this? In late 2007, Demos and Make Your Mark surveyed 50 specialists including entrepreneurs, business leaders, academics and other thought-leaders to help shape this publication. We asked 'what and who will shape the future face of enterprise?' Some of these specialists' viewpoints have been included in this work to present a perspective from the people at the heart of creating an enterprise culture in the UK. All of the viewpoints can be read in full at www.makeyourmark.org.uk/ policy/ future_face_of_enterprise. The responses confirmed that an exciting and vibrant movement is indeed under way. It is diverse, growing and extending its reach in order to create new types of business in new neighbourhoods, new environments and new forms of commerce.

This collection steps back and provides a picture of enterprise today. The essays in the collection describe the different ways in which entrepreneurial culture can affect organisational and product development, the shape of enterprise in the UK, the challenges that we are likely to face in years to come, as well as the mindsets that will be useful in shaping the future. They highlight the business opportunities that arise from developments in web 2.0 technologies, environmental technologies, corporate social responsibility and good business. A concluding chapter brings it all together to ask what all of this might mean for the future of enterprise in Britain.

Notes

1 Foreword by G Brown in HM Treasury, *Enterprise Britain: A modern approach to meeting the enterprise challenge* (London: HM Treasury, Nov 2002).

2 G Mulgan and Perri 6, *The New Enterprise Culture* (London: Demos, 1996).

3 Now called the Department for Business, Enterprise and Regulatory Reform (the use of the word 'enterprise' in the title is perhaps indicative of progress made).

4 The Global Entrepreneurship Monitor (GEM) 2006 reported that, actually, the average start-up cost was £15,000 for men and £7,250 for women. See R Harding, *Global Entrepreneurship Monitor* (London: London Business School, 2006).

5 SC Parker, *The Economics of Self-employment and Entrepreneurship* (New York: Cambridge University Press, 2007); B Bjerke, *Understanding Entrepreneurship* (Cheltenham, UK, and Northampton, MA: Edward Elgar, 2007).

6 P Cilliers, *Complexity and Postmodernism* (New York: Routledge, 1998).

7 Parker, *The Economics of Self-employment and Entrepreneurship*.

8 R Huggins and N Williams, 'Enterprise and public policy: a review of Labour government intervention in the United Kingdom', discussion paper 2007-03, University of Sheffield, Aug 2007, see www.shef.ac.uk/management/research/papers/abstracts/2007-03.html (accessed 12 Jun 2008); Parker, *The Economics of Self-employment and Entrepreneurship*; A Lundstrom and LA Stevenson, *Entrepreneurship Policy: Theory and practice* (Boston: Springer, 2005).

9 Office for National Statistics, *Small- and Medium-sized Enterprise (SME) Statistics for the UK 2006* (London: ONS, Aug 2007).

10   R Harding, *Global Entrepreneurship Monitor* (London: London Business School, 2006); Huggins and Williams, 'Enterprise and public policy'.

11   Harding, *Global Entrepreneurship Monitor*.

12   Ibid.

13   Department for Work and Pensions, *In Work, Better Off: Next steps to full employment*, Cm 7130 (Norwich: HMSO, Jul 2007), available at www.dwp.gov.uk/welfarereform/in-work-better-off/in-work-better-off.pdf (accessed 17 Jun 2008).

14   Office of the Third Sector, *Social Enterprise Action Plan: Scaling new heights* (London: Cabinet Office, 2006), see www.cabinetoffice.gov.uk/third_sector/social_enterprise/action_plan.aspx (accessed 12 Jun 2008).

Section summaries

Shawnee Keck and Alessandra Buonfino

Section 1: Economic geographies of enterprise

Freed from a dependence on heavy raw materials, in theory business can now take place anywhere in postindustrial Britain. And it does. The new clusters of enterprise centre on ideas, not coal, steel or cotton, and they are harder to pin on the map.

Peter Day

This section looks at the economic and geographical impact of enterprise on places and countries. With economic production and distribution no longer easy to identify, we are increasingly dealing in the currency of knowledge and ideas in a 'flat' world. In chapter 1, economist David Audretsch explains how small firms, some of which were founded by former employees with experimental ideas, have become the catalysts and multipliers of innovative knowledge by turning ideas into profitable ventures. Audretsch highlights that without small firms, large organisations could not develop all the ideas they generate. It is innovative entrepreneurs and knowledge spill-over that will move concepts ahead, using collective capital from the core and from other partners. This collaboration is at the heart of a global boom in small business. The future face of enterprise should recognise that while good business ideas can come from anywhere, they will only prosper in an environment that supports open innovation and networks of support for those starting out.

Broadcaster Peter Day takes a journey around Britain to draw a map of the most enterprising places and hotspots across the country. He describes how business is no longer physically located only in the metropoles; it is dispersed out to the regions and even further afield. Technology spreads opportunities down to the very micro level showing how the knowledge spill-over is really occurring in the UK. In Cambridge's Silicon Fen alone,

1,300 business were created within the last 30 years. Regional clustering is replicating partnerships and leveraging capital to generate hubs of science, technology and all the businesses that supply them.

Audretsch writes about the difficult task of shaking up and exciting people into believing that they can change the future. The goal of policy in the next phase becomes making progress on the 'soft' barriers to entry – such as confidence, communication and acceptance of risk. Carl Schramm and Robert Litan from the US-based Kauffman Foundation provocatively argue that an anti-enterprise culture accounts for 'economic sluggishness' across Europe. They set out a need to follow the examples of the few EU countries that have stimulated enterprise successfully.

Viewpoints in this section are given from Rebecca Harding, Delta Economics ltd; Arif Ahmed and Kubair Shirazee, Ikonami; Simon Woodroffe, YO! Sushi; and Kulveer Taggar, Auctomatic.com.

Section 2: The business of social change

Business and enterprise have exciting potential when it comes to addressing the big challenges facing society (challenges such as climate change or poverty). Budding environmentalists and social entrepreneurs are not short of new ideas to address fundamental environmental and social challenges. But the real test is getting these ideas scaled up to achieve impact.[1]

Social and environmental transformations are happening, and the social movements of the past are becoming the businesses of the future. Without the devoted radicals, and the 'disruptive' behaviour of social and environmental entrepreneurs and visionaries who have worked tirelessly on the margins for so long, there would not have been much progress. The growing interest in the potential of business contributing to social change is expressed clearly in this collection through the viewpoints of Ronald Cohen, chairman, Bridges Ventures and The Portland Trust, Jeremy Leggett of Solarcentury, John Bird, founder of *The Big Issue*, and Mel Lambert, former Group HR Director for IVECO Fiat, entrepreneur and consultant.

Often, social change can really happen through partnerships between big business and citizen entrepreneurs. As John Elkington argues in chapter 4, partnerships are extremely important: individual social entrepreneurs are unlikely to have a huge impact on their own, and similarly, large organisations need small, creative businesses to help with innovative social responses.

Social change and business change are also being aided by technological advances, as Jim Lawn describes. Social media tools are enabling prospective entrepreneurs to exchange information and engage with each other. Lawn reveals how technologically equipped masses across the globe have taken over parts of production and inserted themselves into research and development, design and marketing. Then Lawn describes the long tail of democracy and economics and the way that social media is not only connecting long-lost primary school sweethearts, but also offering immediate and transparent feedback on services and goods in a global market. He shows how the future will turn the idea of scale upside down as niche markets turn more profit collectively than mass consumption.

Peter Grigg and Joanne Lacey demonstrate how the future face of enterprise could well be centred around notions of 'good business'. The Ethical Purchasing Index (EPI) values the total value of the 'ethical sector' at £32.3 billion in the UK and growing, with the average household expenditure on ethical goods up £664 per year (almost double the amount in 2002).[2] This emerging market is big enough to have grabbed the attention and passions of both young employees and young entrepreneurs. In a world where we hear of the demand for values-driven businesses that act with integrity and fairness, the new breed of employees and entrepreneurs are in a unique position to use their enterprising talent.

Section 3: Enterprise skills and mindsets

The third section of this collection examines skills and mindsets that will contribute to the future face of enterprise. What role does enterprise play in the workplace, in communities, and in addressing inequality?

In chapter 7, Gordon Frazer, UK MD of Microsoft, gives an insight into a global corporation as it comes to grips with cultural changes necessary to accommodate more enterprising employees. Re-thinking the way employees are integrated into generating new ideas or improving on current products is restructuring internal building design, adding team visioning sessions to the work week, and allowing for internships in partner businesses. Hiring for passion, in addition to technical skill, commits the corporation to changing its management paradigm. Enterprising staff is placed at the heart of future business growth and success.

Duncan O'Leary and Paul Skidmore, in chapter 8, argue that career structures and business development have changed – but still largely to the detriment of those at the low-paid end of the labour market. Those with low skills are *both* likely to experience job insecurity in conventional careers and fewer chances to start successful enterprises. The authors explore how policy might connect the learning, enterprise and work agendas – and how else policy could help level the playing field.

During the course of the research for this collection many people highlighted the need for role models for the younger generation. In chapter 9, Tim Campbell and Shawnee Keck examine the potential for enterprise to change the lives of young people who are not being offered much else. Examining the personal experience of enterprise for young people at risk shows that it can make a significant difference to their aspirations. Building on their drive for independence and self-confidence, enterprise training is explored as an option for a new economically excluded group of disadvantaged young people – to inspire them, and raise their aspirations and expectations for the future.

Yet while it is recognised that enterprising behaviours and skills may indeed help young people in their future career decisions, what do these 'soft' skills look like? Based on his seminal work on mindsets, Howard Gardner identifies five types of mind that we should be cultivating for the future to buttress enterprise.

The chapters in this section are supported by the viewpoints of Martha Lane Fox, co-founder of Lastminute.com; Kyle Whitehill, Vodafone UK; Iqbal Wahhab, The Glorious Group; Derek Browne, Entrepreneurs in Action; Linda Austin, Swanlea School, Business and Enterprise College; and Gita Patel, Stargate Capital Investment Group.

Notes

1 G Mulgan with R Ali, R Halkett and B Sanders, *In and Out of Sync: The challenge of growing social innovations* (London: National Endowment for Science, Technology and the Arts (NESTA) and the Young Foundation, 2007).

2 Co-operative Bank, *The Ethical Consumerism Report 2007* (Manchester: Co-operative Bank, 2007), see www.goodwithmoney.co.uk/images/pdf/ethical_consumer _report_2007.pdf (accessed 12 Jun 2008).

SECTION 1: ECONOMIC GEOGRAPHIES OF ENTERPRISE

Economic activity in the UK was once relatively clean and easy to identify but the economic and geographical dynamics of enterprise are changing. Where will enterprise be at the heart of a thriving UK in the twenty-first century?

I am the founder of the World Entrepreneurship Summit 2008 and of Delta Economics and the coordinator of Global Entrepreneurship Monitor UK so I speak as both an entrepreneur and a researcher.

The challenges that we face as a world over the next century are so substantial that we cannot afford to ignore them. We need to harness the innate adaptive capacity of an economy or society in order to create wealth. Who better to do this than the people themselves: the people who are the agents of change – not governments, not businesses, but entrepreneurs.

The changes we will need to make to meet these challenges will not only be perpetual, but also paradigmatic. Technological change as an example is rapid and global. Competitive strategy cannot be seen any more as a linear process from conception through to implementation. Individuals in emerging countries as well as the older, more developed economies are able to access the global labour market from their homes and not just from the workplace. In the words of Ben Verwaayen, the CEO of British Telecom, 'It takes a dog, a chair and a computer to be part of the global economic order. The dog to wake you up, the chair to sit down on and the computer to log-in to the world.' This is a wake-up call for policy makers, especially in the developed world, to ensure that they are maintaining and developing the workforce skills to compete with the rapidly improving skills base of the emerging economies and, critically, to have the flexibility to work in an increasingly entrepreneurial way.

Increasingly though, as the world economic order develops, it is no longer adequate purely to think of wealth creation in economic terms. Increasing numbers are excluded as global inequalities grow and as the environmental and climate change consequences of our activities become apparent. The world's largest businesses must think not just in terms of how to be efficient, but also in terms of how to minimise their impact on the environments and communities in which they are based while maximising the effectiveness with which they manage their operations.

Whole regions are currently excluded from the global economic order. Development such as the basic steps for establishing a rule of law, designing social welfare services, and developing communities that participate as equals are just some of the mammoth tasks before them. More than this, as the case of China in particular suggests, even when countries do develop rapidly, their energy consumption and growth creates irreversible changes to the environment, which cannot be ignored.

As a result of all this, we cannot as analysts, commentators and business leaders afford to be dogmatic about our approach to entrepreneurship. It is no exaggeration to say that the role of entrepreneurs in creating wealth is pivotal. However, we now need to turn our attention to the role of entrepreneurs in sustaining that wealth and extending it to the communities and to the issues that are currently excluded from the mainstream debate.

For this, we need to understand that entrepreneurs fall into a 'genus' with common characteristics that have been the drivers of change throughout human history. But we equally need to understand that different 'species' of entrepreneurs serve different purposes at different times in our development. Maybe the time has come for large and small companies to think in terms of the social and environmental impact of their operations and, hence, to think about entrepreneurship in its broadest sense as a means of addressing how to meet that triple bottom line.

1 Dynamite comes in small packages

David Audretsch

One of the most fundamental policy issues confronting Western Europe and North America during the postwar era was the perceived trade-off between the economic efficiency of large corporate firms on the one hand, and the benefits of political and economic decentralisation of small business on the other. There appeared to be an inevitable trade-off between the gains in productive efficiency from increased concentration in large organisations and gains from competition, and implicitly democracy, from decentralising policies that promoted broad ownership.

The policy response was to constrain the freedom of large corporate firms to contract – through public ownership, regulation, and competition or antitrust policy. At the time, it seemed that there were glaring differences in the policy approaches to this apparent trade-off being taken by different countries: France and Sweden resorted to government ownership of private business; the Netherlands and Germany tended to emphasise regulation; other countries such as the US placed a greater emphasis on anti-trust. In reality, most countries relied on elements of all three policy instruments. But, while the particular mechanisms may have varied across countries, they were all, in fact, manifestations of a singular policy approach – an attempt to restrict and restrain the power of the large corporation. What seemed like a disparate set of policies at the time appears, in retrospect, to comprise a remarkably singular policy approach.

Western economists and policy makers of the day were nearly unanimous in their acclaim for large-scale enterprises. It is an irony of history that this consensus mirrored a remarkably similar gigantism embedded in Soviet doctrine, fuelled by the writings of Marx and ultimately implemented by the iron fist of

Stalin. This was the era of mass production when economies of scale seemed to be the decisive factor in determining efficiency. This was the world so colourfully described by JK Galbraith in his 1956 *American Capitalism: A theory of countervailing power*,[1] in which big business was held in check by big labour and by big government. This was the 1950s, the era of the man in the grey flannel suit, David Riesman's *The Lonely Crowd*[2] and William H Whyte's *The Organization Man*,[3] when virtually every major social and economic institution acted to reinforce the stability and predictability needed for mass production.

Thus, while a heated debate emerged about which approach best promoted large-scale production and simultaneously constrained the ability of large corporations to exert market power, there was much less debate about public policy towards small business and entrepreneurship. The only issue was whether public policy makers should simply allow small firms to disappear as a result of their inefficiency or intervene to preserve them solely on social and political grounds. Those who perceived small firms to contribute significantly to growth, job creation and competitiveness were few and far between.

In the postwar era, small firms and entrepreneurship were viewed as a luxury, perhaps needed to ensure the decentralisation of decision making, but obtained only at a cost to efficiency. Certainly the systematic empirical evidence, gathered from both Europe and North America, documented a sharp trend towards a decreased role of small firms during the postwar period. Public policy towards small firms generally reflected the view that they were a drag on economic efficiency and growth, generated lower-quality jobs, and were generally on the way to becoming less important to the economy, if not threatened by long-term extinction. Eventually, some countries, such as the former Soviet Union, but also Sweden and France, adapted the policy stance of allowing small firms to gradually disappear and account for a smaller share of economic activity. The stance of the United States reflected a long-term political and social valuation of small firms that seemed to reach back to the Jeffersonian traditions of the country. Thus, the public policy towards small business in the US was oriented towards actively preserving what was considered to be inefficient enterprises, which, if left unprotected, might otherwise become extinct. Even advocates of small business agreed that small firms were less efficient than big companies. These advocates were willing to sacrifice a modicum of efficiency, however, because of all the other contributions – moral, political and otherwise – made by small business to society. Small business policy was thus 'preservationist' in character.

New economies, same old problems

But things were about to change and in remarkable ways; small enterprises may have proved useful to the economy after all. In the new models of economic growth theory, ideas and creativity, or what economists called knowledge, were identified as replacing factories as the driving force underlying economic growth. Knowledge was viewed as being a particularly potent force for growth, because ideas were assumed to flow out like effervescent fountains, providing a bubbly stream of insights, information and inspiration that would trigger innovations and productivity in other firms and people.

But it didn't quite happen like that, or at least not as smoothly and as frictionless as portrayed in the elegant new models. Even as Europe began losing the comparative advantage in physical capital in the 1990s, it expected it would be well poised to thrive with a knowledge-based economy. The Nordic countries in particular, but also Northern Europe more generally, ranked among the world's leaders in terms of the most common measures of knowledge.

However, the inability of knowledge leaders, such as Sweden, to prosper in the new global economy was so striking that it became referred to as the *Swedish Paradox*. Even with the highest rates of investment in research, human capital and culture in the world, Sweden exhibited surprisingly low business growth rates and rising unemployment. And it was not just Sweden; after seeing similar trends, economists adapted the label to the European Union, and it became a *European Paradox*.

The problem is that the products of private or university research and development – the ideas, creativity, intuition and insights – do not automatically spill-over to become new products or new techniques. Rather, what we call the 'knowledge filter' poses a barrier between investments in knowledge that have a *potential* commercial value and knowledge that is actually taken to market. This filter impedes investment of viable research from spilling over into commercialisation leading to the so-called Swedish or European Paradox.

Meanwhile, small firms appeared to be at least as incompatible with the knowledge-based economy as they were in the factory-based economy. The most prevalent theory of innovation in economics, the model of the knowledge production function, suggested that knowledge-generating inputs in the form of research and development were a prerequisite to generating innovative outputs like software and medicine. Conventional wisdom would also have predicted that increased globalisation would present a more hostile environment to small business. Caves argued in 1982 that the additional costs of globalisation, which would be incurred by small business 'constitute an important reason for expecting that foreign investment will be mainly an activity of large firms'.[4] With their limited and meagre investments in research and development (R&D), at least in absolute terms, new and small firms did not seem to possess sufficient knowledge capabilities to be competitive in a knowledge-based economy.

Local networks, local knowledge

However, appearances were wrong. The power of innovation emerges, somehow, and our research shows that the filter generates opportunities for individuals, or teams of people, to take that information with them and start a new business. If people are not able to pursue and implement their ideas and vision within the context of an existing firm or organisation, they may need to start a new firm – and become entrepreneurs. Not only can they be an option to force the stalled knowledge filter but, as both Zoltan Acs and I surprisingly found, in 1988 and

1990, small firms actually provided the engines of innovative activity, at least in certain industries.[5]

But how do innovative firms with little or no R&D get their knowledge inputs? This question becomes particularly relevant for small and new firms that undertake little R&D themselves, yet contribute considerable activity in newly emerging industries such as biotechnology and computer software. Incredibly, the new economic geography of knowledge has a very local factor to it. Research spill-overs and spin-offs (the side effects and leftovers of production) are shared through third-party firms or research institutions, such as universities, within the same regional area.

Economically viable knowledge then spreads out from the laboratories to nearby new and small firms to generate and sustain a whole product community. Additionally, Jaffe (1989), Audretsch with Feldman (1996) and Audretsch with Stephan (1996) provided findings suggesting that knowledge spill-overs are geographically bounded and localised within proximity to the knowledge source.[6] None of these studies, however, identified the mechanisms which actually transmit the knowledge spill-over; rather, the spill-overs were implicitly assumed to automatically exist (or fall like Manna from heaven), but only within these geographically bounded areas.

Knowledge spill-over: grease for the creative wheels

The knowledge spill-over theory of entrepreneurship suggests that contexts that are rich in knowledge, ideas and creativity will tend to generate more entrepreneurial opportunities. A consequence of globalisation has been to shift the comparative advantage of the leading developed countries from physical capital to knowledge, which in turn spawns pervasive entrepreneurial opportunities. However, only those areas that are able not only to invest in creativity but also to penetrate the knowledge-filter by facilitating this entrepreneurship will be best put to take advantage of the opportunities afforded by globalisation. If a country cannot stimulate this self-replicating system, it will fall as yet another victim to outsourcing and offshoring. It is the entrepreneurs who generate a return to society on its precious investments in intelligent, thoughtful, intuitive and creative people, a very efficient role for small, agile firms to play.

The knowledge spill-over theory of entrepreneurship was supported by analysing variations in start-up rates across different industries. In particular, industries with a greater investment in new knowledge also exhibited higher start-up rates while industries with less investment also exhibited a lower start-up rate. Thus, compelling evidence was provided suggesting that entrepreneurship is an intra-community response to opportunities created but not exploited by the incumbent firms. This contests the view that entrepreneurial opportunities are rare and that only a unique combination of specific individual characteristics and attributes will influence the cognitive process underlying the entrepreneurial decision to start a firm. Rather, the knowledge spill-over theory of entrepreneurship explicitly identifies an important source of opportunities – investments in knowledge and ideas made by firms and universities that are not completely commercialised. In 2005, a comprehensive study with colleagues at the Max Planck Institute[7] found that regions rich in knowledge generated a greater amount of entrepreneurial opportunities than regions with impoverished knowledge. This confirmed that entrepreneurial opportunities are not chance occurrences but, rather, they are systematically related to the knowledge context.

As part of this theory, I proposed shifting the unit of observation away from firms to individuals, such as scientists, engineers or other knowledge workers – agents with endowments of new economic knowledge. The question then becomes: 'How can economic agents with a given endowment of new knowledge best appropriate the returns from that knowledge?' If the scientist or engineer can pursue the new idea and roughly appropriate the expected value of that knowledge within his or her organisational structure, he or she has no reason to leave the firm. On the other hand, if the scientist or engineer places a greater value on his or her ideas than does the decision-making bureaucracy of the incumbent firm, he or she may choose to start a new firm to appropriate the value of this knowledge.

Entrepreneurial links to growth

Entrepreneurship has emerged as a vital organisational form for economic growth because it provides the missing link between *potential* products and actualisation[8] in the process of economic growth. By serving as a conduit for the spill-over of knowledge, entrepreneurship is a mechanism by which investments, both private and public, generate a multiple social return, in terms of economic growth and job creation.

In addition to labour, physical capital and knowledge capital, the endowment of *entrepreneurship capital* also matters for generating economic growth.[9] Entrepreneurship capital refers to the capacity for spatial units to generate new enterprises.[10]

The entrepreneurship capital of an economy or a society refers to the institutions, culture and historical context that is conducive to the creation of new firms. This involves a number of aspects: the social acceptance of entrepreneurial behaviour; individuals who are willing to take on the risk of creating new firms; and the activity of bankers and venture capital agents willing to share the risks and benefits involved. Hence, entrepreneurial success reflects a number of different legal, institutional and social factors and forces. Taken together, these forces constitute the *entrepreneurship capital* of an economy, which creates a capacity for entrepreneurial activity and reinforces a broader entrepreneurial culture. By including measures of entrepreneurship capital along with the traditional factors of physical and knowledge capital and labour in a production function model estimating economic growth, we found pervasive and compelling econometric evidence suggesting that entrepreneurship capital also contributes to economic growth.

Promoting entrepreneurship, a reversal for the future

With the rediscovery of the role of entrepreneurship, it is not surprising there has been a reawakening in policy. This time, the rets are more precise and there is better recognition of exactly what grease we are interested in leveraging. It is important to distinguish entrepreneurship policy from traditional small- and medium-sized enterprise (SME) policy.[11] The key difference is the breadth of policy orientation and instruments. While SME policy has a focus on the existing stock of SMEs, entrepreneurship policy is more encompassing in that it includes *potential* entrepreneurs as well as the existing stock. This suggests that entrepreneurship policy is more focused on the process of change, regardless of the organisational unit, whereas SME policy is focused exclusively on the unit of analysis. Entrepreneurship policy also has a greater sensitivity to the frameworks or environmental conditions that shape the individual decision-making process of entrepreneurs.

While SME policy is primarily concerned with one organisational level – the enterprise – entrepreneurship policy encompasses multiple units of organisation and analysis. These range from the individual to the enterprise, and to the cluster or network, which might involve an industry or sectoral dimension, or a spatial dimension, such as a district, city, region, or even an entire country. Just as each of these levels is an important target for policy, the interactions and linkages across these disparate levels are also important. In this sense, entrepreneurship policy tends to be more systemic than SME policy. However, it is important to emphasise that SME policy still remains at the core of entrepreneurship policy.

Even with the need for a broad approach to entrepreneurship policy, the mandate for entrepreneurship policy has generally emerged from what would superficially appear to be two opposite directions. One direction emanates from the failure of the traditional policy instruments, corresponding to economic models emphasising physical capital – machines to adequately maintain economic growth and employment in globally linked markets. The second push for the entrepreneurship policy mandate comes from the opposite direction: the failure of the so-called new economy policy instruments, corresponding to the models promoting investment into knowledge capital to adequately generate economic growth and employment. Remember the European Paradox, where employment creation and economic growth remain meagre despite world-class levels of human capital and research capabilities, which triggered the Lisbon Proclamation stating that Europe would become the entrepreneurship leader by 2020?

Although coming from opposite directions, both have in common an unacceptable economic performance. In other words, the mandate for entrepreneurship policy is rooted in dissatisfaction – dissatisfaction with the status quo, and in particular with the status quo economic performance. As the initial capital-driven Solow model and the more recent knowledge-driven Romer model have not delivered the expected levels of economic performance by themselves, a mandate for entrepreneurship policy has emerged and begun to diffuse throughout the entire globe.

A number of government-sponsored technology policies in four countries – the UK, Germany, Japan and the US – have triggered the start-up of new firms. The majority of the start-up programmes are targeted towards eliminating particular bottlenecks in the development and financing of new firms. In 1990, Sternberg examined the impact that 70 innovation centres have had on the development of technology-based small firms.[12] He found that the majority of the entrepreneurs gained a number of advantages by locating at an innovation centre. In 1996, he documented how the success of different high-technology clusters, spanning a number of developed countries, is the direct result of *enabling policies*, such as the provision of venture capital or research support.[13] The last decade has seen the emergence of a broad spectrum of enabling policy initiatives that fall outside the jurisdiction of the traditional regulatory agencies.

Whether or not specific policy instruments will work in their particular contexts is not the point. What is striking, however, is the emergence and diffusion of an entirely new public policy approach to generate economic growth – the creation of the entrepreneurial society. It is on this new mantel of the entrepreneurial society that places, ranging from local areas to cities, states and even entire nations, hang their hopes, dreams and aspirations for prosperity and security.

David B Audretsch is director of the Institute for Development Strategies at Indiana University; director of the Entrepreneurship, Growth and Public Policy Group at the Max Planck Institute in Jena, Germany; and a research fellow of the Centre for Economic Policy Research in London.

Viewpoint
Arif Ahmed and Kubair Shirazee, Ikonami

We set up Ikonami in our respective bedrooms back in 1999 because we thought that we could build software better. The first year or so was great; there was a lot of demand for consulting and implementation services. Having advised clients such as the NHS, Argos and Royal Bank of Scotland, we were well placed to deliver. However, the 2000/01 technology crash saw our business effectively disappear overnight. It was during this period that we really cut our business teeth. In many ways this was thanks to our MBA. We walked away from our Mayfair offices, cut staff and changed our business model. Lessons learnt by rote are seldom forgotten; to this day we keep expenses bone trim by 'acting small, thinking big'.

Two years in, and we finally won an NHS project that would change the shape and scale of our business. What started as a web development initiative to manage local NHS staff competences, eventually led to a one-year national Department of Health pilot. While we faced stiff competition from larger global consultancies, our small company approach prevailed. Where others estimated three years to deliver the proposed system, we estimated six months. A major component of our business today remains maintaining this system.

To encourage more entrepreneurship, we need to move away from our current culture of failure and envy. Too many people fear trying something new due to the potential for failure. These people toil 9 to 5 and despise anyone who errs from this arrangement. The same sceptics who doubted our ability to set up and run a business are now the people who claim that they could have done the same had it not been for their mortgages and other commitments.

More children need to be taught that 9 to 5 is not the only option available posteducation. If Britain is to remain a competitive, dynamic economy it really needs to promote alternative working models seriously – entrepreneurship, portfolio careers, job sharing and flexible hours. Without offering advice in these areas, Britain will remain in an industrial age paradigm while trying to tackle knowledge working era problems.

Notes

1   JK Galbraith, *American Capitalism: A theory of countervailing power* (Boston: Houghton Mifflin, 1952).

2   D Riesman, *The Lonely Crowd: A study of the American changing character* (New Haven: Yale University Press, 1953).

3   WH Whyte, *The Organization Man* (New York: Simon Schuster, 1956).

4   RE Caves, *Multinational Enterprise and Economic Analysis* (Cambridge: Cambridge University Press, 1982).

5   D Audretsch, 'Innovation in large and small firms: an empirical analysis', *American Economic Review* 78, no 4 (Sep 1988); D Audretsch with ZJ Acs, *The Economics of Small Firms: A European challenge* (Norwell, MA, and Dordrecht, the Netherlands: Kluwer Academic Publishers, 1990).

6   A Jaffe, 'Real effects of academic research', *American Economic Review* 79, no 5 (1989); D Audretsch with M Feldman, 'R&D spillovers and the geography of innovation and production', *American Economic Review* 86, no 3 (1996); D Audretsch with P Stephan, 'Company scientist locational links: the case of biotechnology', *American Economic Review* 86, no 3 (1996).

7   ZJ Acs et al, *The Knowledge Spillover Theory of Entrepreneurship*, Discussion Papers on Entrepreneurship, Growth and Public Policy 2005-27 (Jena, Germany: Max Planck Institute of Economics, Group for Entrepreneurship, Growth and Public Policy, 2005).

8   SY Lee, R Florida and ZJ Acs, 'Creativity and entrepreneurship: a regional analysis of new firm formation', *Regional Studies* 38 (2004).

9   D Audretsch and M Keilbach, 'Entrepreneurship capital – determinants and impact', CEPR Discussion Paper 4905 (London: Centre for Economic Policy Research, 2005).

10 The concept of social capital added a social component to the traditional factors shaping economic growth and prosperity. Together with Max Keilbach and Erik Lehmann at the Max Planck Institute, we suggest that what has been called social capital in the entrepreneurship literature may actually be a more specific sub-component, which they introduce as entrepreneurship capital.

11 A Lundstrom and L Stevenson, *Entrepreneurship Policy for the Future: On the road to entrepreneurship policy* (Örebro: Swedish Foundation for Small Business Research, 2002).

12 R Sternberg, 'The impact of innovation centers on small technology-based firms: the example of the Federal Republic of Germany', *Small Business Economics* 2 (1990).

13 R Sternberg, 'Technology policies and growth of regions: evidence from four countries', *Small Business Economics* 8 (1996).

2 Putting enterprise on the map

Peter Day

Geography is about maps, but so is economics. Once it was easy to map enterprise in Britain: it was marked out by factory chimneys. Freed from a dependence on heavy raw materials, in theory business can now take place anywhere in postindustrial Britain. And it does. The new clusters of enterprise centre on ideas, not coal, steel or cotton, and they are harder to pin on the map.

Location, naturally, has a huge impact on how businesses start and thrive. The ancient silence of the great mediaeval monasteries smothers the realisation that they were once hectic centres of activity when wool was one of Britain's prime raw materials. Stand in the quietness of the Severn valley at Ironbridge in Shropshire, the first iron bridge across any river, a breathtaking example of the fearlessness of the new technologists of the time. All around are the very beginnings of the industrial revolution of the early eighteenth century: the conjunction of iron, coal and shipping.

At the same time cotton was replacing wool, the mills of Lancashire became some of the first factories in the world, made possible by a succession of mechanical inventions and modifications. There was a rush of connectivity in this new mass production age. Eighteenth-century canal entrepreneurs got their capital back in two years, a rate of return unequalled until recently; now we see cargo ships paying back at similar rates because of the China boom. For a golden century, Britain was the innovative centre of the world. Inventions had wonderful timeliness.

The chance discovery of flexible steel in the Forest of Dean came just as the first mobile steam engines were breaking up the cast iron rails they ran on. This invention was also all about a different type of networking; you could say the Railway Age was the internet bubble of its time. So important was that new technology that in 1845, the just-established magazine *The Economist* changed its name to include the *Railway Monitor*. But few if any investors made money out of the railway mania of the mid 1800s, they saw huge share losses between 1845 and 1855. Just as railway investment left us with a network that changed the shape of nineteenth-century Britain, in much the same way, the internet infrastructure may be disrupting business now.

It is always worth thinking of the past when we examine the future. Britain was so advanced for a time in the nineteenth century that eclipse by latecomers was almost inevitable and so rose Germany and the USA. And here we are in the twenty-first century, with a very different business map of Britain, and a very different set of products and competitors. Invention and reinvention used to be merely the starting point for a company. Now (we are told) it has become the continuing lifeblood of a business: in a consumer world preoccupied with novelty, new ideas are the only differentiator. A company that does not innovate is dead; innovation is at the heart of enterprise, and enterprise is the way countries flourish. This disruption that enterprise brings makes the business of the UK difficult to plot, however. There are few clear statistics on the shape and size of enterprise in Britain now, and few factory chimneys to help indicate where it is. So we will have to map it with landmarks and revenue. When we open the door, we find a country still undergoing profound changes in the shape and size of its business landscape.

Let's start on a positive note. Amidst all the adjustment, the UK still punches quite above its weight. Britain is still a place where the pursuit of new ideas is a much respected activity. On a global basis, tiny Britain undertakes 5 per cent of all the research and publishes 12 per cent of the scientific papers, second only to the USA in citations, which is one way of measuring international eminence. Only the USA has had more scientific Nobel Prize winners in the years since 1970. And, let's not forget, Britain has one huge business advantage, the proprietorship of the world business language.

Cambridge University made the first commercial computer in the world for the visionary J Lyons confectionery company in 1945. But whatever happened to the UK computer industry, and to J Lyons? What happened to the BBC Microcomputer (the first mass-selling British machine for the home) and to Acorn, the Cambridge company which made it? Don't worry, not everything has been lost. While nothing remains of the machine-making part of the British computer industry, out of the ruins, Cambridge has become a significant software centre.

Beyond that, though, the difficulties begin. On the whole, the UK fails to turn all this brainstorming into big commercial success. Japan, the USA and Germany are well ahead of Britain on the measurement of patents granted per head of population. And when it comes to research and development (which is where ideas are really turned into practical products and services) Britain spends only half as much on R&D as Sweden does. Japan, USA, Germany, France and Canada are also well ahead on R&D spending as a proportion of GDP or the total national income. Why do we lag behind on this apparently crucial measure of innovation and enterprise? The deficit seems largely due to a lack of investment by business.

The *Mittelstand*, medium-sized private companies which make up such a significant part of the German economy, are often run by engineers who are obsessed with buying the most up-to-date machinery for their factories, just as a matter of course. In the UK, accountants dominate top management and capital spending in Britain still requires a very assured rate of return. This may explain why British productivity lags behind many of our industrial competitors. Low-wage economies such as Britain have less need than high-wage economies to invest in equipment that replaces expensive workers. Compared with competing countries, British workers spend much longer hours producing the same amount of stuff.

The UK economy has changed dramatically in the past 20 or 30 years, and all these sober assessments may be overemphasising the decline of the resource and manufacturing past and may underestimate where we are now. As far up as Aberdeen, the old industrial centres are dwindling now. The last of the oil supply companies that long ago outgrew their North Sea origins have followed the exploration industry into the most difficult terrains on earth – or sea. My generation is still burdened with the plodding thinking of manufacturing as the prime mover of an economy. We remember that, in the 1960s, the Labour government's taxation of service industries was somehow improper compared with the horny-handed making of things. If you pay a visit to the acclaimed manufacturing guru Professor Lord Bhattacharyya at the University of Warwick's Manufacturing Group, you'll drive through the carcass of ruined British manufacturing in the West Midlands. While Lord Bhattacharyya's enthusiasm for manufacturing gets world attention, he has had seemingly little impact in his adopted land. Britain makes more cars than it ever did in the days of Rover and Austin, but they do not bear British badges any more. It is apparent; something has changed and we have moved on.

We can start with the usual suspects. London is still the enterprise capital of the UK, a reminder of how important trade is when it comes to enterprise. Even at the height of the intense activity of the northern industrial revolution, the bankers, brokers and traders of the City generated vast amounts of overseas earnings and jobs, many based on international trade. And Britain's dwindling overseas influence has done nothing to diminish activity in London. A combination of international connections, ingenuity, language and a fortunate GMT time zone has reinforced London's importance as an international financial centre, keeping ahead of the developments of international finance as they happen, and reinvigorating London's role as a world city. This attractiveness provides many opportunities for internationally minded people: in particular, the flourishing of the creative, theatre, film, TV and advertising industries, making London a global node of ideas.

But, I have my doubts that London can retain long-term eminence in these industries or in the financial sectors in the face of the rise of the new giant economies in China and India. Sooner or later the centre of economic power is bound to shift eastwards, but the City authorities remain ready for action. To keep up, the enterprise map of London is constantly changing, as any reader of Dickens (or the newspaper property pages) will be aware. Cheap rents in fringe properties encouraged the dot.com entrepreneurs to move to Shoreditch and Hackney in East London in the 1990s. Newly rampant hedge funds and private equity investors have no need of the vast dealing rooms of the Square Mile or Docklands, so they have moved finance to Mayfair and the West End. It will be interesting to see which locations survive the changes. The latest Global Entrepreneurship Monitor says the Southwest has outdone London this last study, 7.1 per cent of adults are engaged in enterprise compared with London's 6 per cent; these numbers fluctuate but the shifting tides are occurring.[1]

There is not only just a change in the physical landscape of enterprise, but also the institutional landscape. The rise of the knowledge economy has uprooted the map of Britain, and universities, once backwaters of business activity, are now at the centre of intensifying clusters of business development. Imperial College London has a company called Imperial Innovations quoted on the stock market, with stakes in 60 companies spun out from university research. Other universities have built similar clusters of enterprise around them, either deliberately or by happy accident, and that brings us back to the Cambridge phenomenon. In the so-called Silicon Fen, some 1,300 companies have sprung up over 30 years, largely drawing on expertise in the university. Most are small, but even the largest companies license their technology or have their production outsourced. This means that the big ideas of ARM – the Bluetooth chip-maker Cambridge Silicon Radio – and the search experts at Autonomy have not led to large-scale domestic employment. And even if a company has got big ideas with accompanying factories, would the planners ever allow the Cambridge countryside to be covered with manufacturing facilities?

The micro map of Cambridge enterprise is an extraordinary cat's cradle of connections centring on just a handful of entrepreneurial personalities. It is the envy of other places, and not just in Britain. But the university earns little direct revenue from this slew of wealth creation, by way of royalties or shareholdings in local companies. It is government policy to encourage universities to sweat their assets by creating businesses out of the innovations in their labs. Just as well, an engineer with brilliant ideas may not be the best person to turn an invention into a business. In Cambridge there is vigorous debate about whether it's practical to expect many university-hatched businesses to prosper. Some experts argue that the best business ideas emerge from the friction of daily contact with customers and the real world, a reality from which most academics are shielded. Many Cambridge companies have been created through the consultancies that have sprung up around the city. They provide the urgency and business pragmatism that the university labs seem often to lack. And if ex-students trained in the university go on to make fortunes elsewhere and come back to fund large endowments (as they do in the USA), then the university eventually benefits from the ideas it generates.

Many other university clusters now dot the enterprise map of Britain. Oxford is particularly strong in chemistry; Edinburgh in medical research, micro and optical electronics and bio informatics; Dundee has computing and biomedicine; Manchester produces biotech and computer software; there are many more. York is proud to have started the Science City concept, which concentrates company research efforts close to the expanding campus. The idea has now spread to Newcastle, Birmingham, Bristol, Manchester and Nottingham as well. They all insist this deliberate cluster building is proof that they aren't merely claiming they're 'scientific' and waiting for the incomers to relocate. With all this energy, only 4 per cent of graduates are entrepreneurs; we have room to grow.

In keeping with this pattern, other cluster themes have formed around prominent firms: a grouping of 500 small aerospace businesses in the South West attached to Airbus and Rolls-Royce. In Cornwall, the visionary Eden Project has brought hope and economic revival to a long-depressed area, together with a new network of business suppliers to the project. There is the remarkable bunch of engineering businesses based on motor racing, often in tiny towns clustered around Silverstone race track in Northamptonshire; with more than 2,000 companies, and 40,000 workers, the world-class companies are pretty invisible unless you look for them. There are 557,000 businesses in rural areas of England alone, which make up 30 per cent of the total. The annual revenue of these firms has gone up to £320 billion, an increase of 10 per cent in five years. Did we notice?

More prominent is the activity in Big Pharma, an industry in which Britain has huge influence. Great laboratory clusters loom out of the countryside; GlaxoSmithKline in Stevenage and Pfizer on the marshes at Sandwich in Kent are employers of thousands of highly skilled doctors and scientists from all over the world. They are working to find cutting-edge cures in state-of-the-art facilities and calling on a very willing supply of research and staff from our universities. Among the pioneering discoveries in Sandwich is the mistaken invention of Pfizer's Viagra; the company was actually seeking an improved treatment for angina.

And don't forget how the small market towns between Reading and Bristol have been transformed by their inclusion in what is called Silicon Corridor. We can see office building after building carrying unfamiliar but potent international brand names with unknown world-class software companies working away up tiny alleys. They are all close to Heathrow airport to serve their clients anywhere in the world.

While it's hard to recognise immediately, there are many more places with surprising things happening behind closed doors. Blink and you'll miss the tiny companies with global networks, thanks to the open source movement, for example. The internet and broadband connections are banishing distance as a constraint; in theory it is now possible for a start-up business to have a global customer base from day one.

Every country in the world longs for its own version of Silicon Valley, California, the epitome of Darwinian capitalism evolving at warp speed. But few places anywhere have anything like that conjunction of bright people or venture capitalists and other risk-hungry investors. All of this combines to generate the intense infrastructure of super-experienced people and willing capital moving like lightning in pursuit of a really good idea. Andy Bechtolsheim of Sun Microsystems was so convinced by an early morning pitch from two young soon-to-be founders he met one day that before he hurried away, he made out a cheque for a $100,000 stake in the fledgling company 'Google', a business which at that stage did not even have a bank account.

That sort of thing – the sheer thrill of business ingenuity – is rather more restrained in Britain, but it does happen here. We may not produce a Google, but who does? The 20-something founders of Innocent Smoothies thought up their business plan on a simple aspiration: they wanted to make something they would want to use (or drink) themselves. Honest insights like that will put innovation in Britain back on the map.

Peter Day has been reporting on business for the BBC since 1974. He now presents In Business *on Radio 4 and* Global Business *for the BBC World Service.*

Viewpoint
Simon Woodroffe, Founder of YO! Sushi

I left school at the age of 16 and spent 30 years in the entertainment business. In the 1990s, I pioneered television deals to show huge international rock concerts worldwide, including Nelson Mandela concerts, shows for Amnesty International and the Prince's Trust concerts. In 1997, I founded YO! Sushi, the sushi restaurant featuring a conveyor belt. Most recently, I was one of the original 'Dragons' on the BBC2's Dragons' Den *making and breaking the dreams of would-be entrepreneurs looking for investment in their business idea.*

I really think our society has been entrepreneurial throughout history. In the eighteenth and nineteenth centuries UK businesses conquered the world. We are not a nation of shopkeepers; we are nation of entrepreneurs. This new attention is a renaissance of old habits. This moment will decide the UK's destiny, and our direction for the next 100 years. We are no longer a manufacturing nation, but a nation of scientists and entrepreneurs who are shaping UK foundations in chemical, biological and engineering businesses.

Invention and science will, in the long term, solve many of the problems of humankind and create the most happiness. Technological progress has helped us make great leaps before. New communications technology has provided a fantastic means of connecting people's thoughts. This is an amazing opportunity. If we put our energy towards more science and innovation, we could imagine a world where every single brain had access to every other brain, and business ideas would take off in no time. It sounds crazy, but it could change business overnight. Look what instant messages did for working from home! Britain needs to see itself as an entrepreneurial nation ready to take advantage of this exciting revival.

The ability to do this depends entirely on education. We have children who at 11 and 13 have great imaginations and live in a world of ideas. Over the next seven years, we then put them through the trauma of the exam system scaring them away from failure. We make them fear that they haven't got what the system asks for, and it kills their confidence. Few realise that they don't need testing and qualifications to succeed. I have virtually no qualifications, but I have some imagination, great enthusiasm and a willingness to use cool technology. We need to make sure that the education system helps to grow ideas rather than stifle them. Invention and science are filled with risk and our children should feel like they are ready to take it on.

Notes
1   R Harding, *Global Entrepreneurship Monitor* (London: London Business School, 2007).

3 Can Europe (

Carl Schramm and Ro'

Last year marked the fiftieth anniversary of the Treaty of ʀ⌐ the agreement that created the European Economic Community, the precursor to today's European Union. Conferences, festivals and summits have been held across the continent to celebrate a half-century of peace and growing cooperation. It now seems almost archaic to think of France and Germany as enemies – an achievement for which European integration, initiated in the wake of the devastation of the Second World War, deserves substantial credit.

In recent years, the EU has expanded eastward to include most of the countries of the former Soviet bloc, and it has also grown in institutional heft. The European Parliament, though toothless in some respects, has established itself as an influential voice on issues of common political concern; the European Central Bank has become a major player in international finance; and the European Court of Justice is of growing importance in international law. Perhaps most impressive has been the introduction of a common currency, the euro, which has reduced the costs of trade and capital flows within Europe and, of late, has risen sharply in value relative to the dollar.

Despite these positive developments, however, there is no avoiding the gloom that has hovered over the anniversary. Most Europeans have decidedly mixed feelings about the EU, and have resisted further integration. In 2005, voters in France and the Netherlands, two countries firmly wedded to the European project, expressed their ambivalence by rejecting a proposed European constitution.

Much of the backlash can be traced to the lacklustre economic performance of most European economies, especially as compared with those of the US and Asia. The countries of the EU have prospered, to be sure, but not nearly as much as

⸁s expected in the heyday of their joint enterprise. Nor ⸲ey alone in their hopes for an integrated, liberalised ⸲nent. In the early 1990s, the economist Lester Thurow of ⸲T wrote a best-selling book, *Head to Head*, in which he ⸲orecast, among other things, that Western Europe would soon overtake the United States economically.[1]

But this never materialised, and now Europe's citizens and political leaders openly worry about the future. Put simply, they wonder: can Europe compete?

Today's 27-member EU is an outgrowth of the European Coal and Steel Community, formed in 1951 with just six members – Germany, France, Italy, Belgium, the Netherlands and Luxembourg. The early focus of the community was on eliminating barriers to the cross-border flow of goods, services and capital. The point was to promote trade and growth, but the broader political aim was to reduce the economic tensions that, in the previous 40 years, had contributed to the onset of two European wars.

As an exercise in opening borders, the European project has been a remarkable success, creating a single market that now extends from London and Lisbon to Helsinki and Athens. Today, it is possible, at least in principle, for any citizen of an EU country to work in another EU country. As for the EU's economic performance, here, too, there has been some good news. The unemployment rate in Western European countries (the so-called EU-15), after hovering in the 10 per cent range for most of the 1990s, has dropped steadily to roughly 7 per cent. Inflation has remained low, in the 2 per cent range.

The great disappointment has been lagging growth in living standards. After approaching the American level of per-capita income in the 1980s, Western Europe has since fallen back somewhat (with the exception of booming Ireland). Labour-force productivity, which is the main driver of living standards, has inched forward at less than 1 per cent annually since 2000, compared to a pace of 2.5 per cent in the US. A study published last year by Eurochambres, the European business lobby, concluded that, in terms of its place in the world economy, the 'EU is progressing at an insufficient pace'.[2]

What accounts for the EU's economic sluggishness? In the first place, there is a profound demographic problem. Aging is a far more serious challenge for Europe than for the United States. By 2030, a quarter of Western Europe's population will be at least 65 years old, twice the share of children under 15. Although the birth rate in a few EU member states – France, Denmark, Ireland – has bounced back in recent years, approaching the replacement rate of two-plus children per family, it would have to climb much more in these countries and elsewhere in Europe to offset the rapid increase in the ranks of senior citizens. The US population will also age during this period, with an elderly population comprising close to 20 per cent, still outnumbered by children under 15.

As an economic matter, Europe's aging population will make it much more expensive for governments to finance the pension and health-care benefits that they have promised. To make matters worse, countries with aging populations tend to resist change and, lacking a large supply of young people, fall short in the energy and zeal needed for innovation. Still worse, if continental Europe fails to provide opportunities for its most ambitious young residents, they will continue their already substantial migration across the English Channel – to the healthy economies of Great Britain and Ireland – thus making it even more difficult for their countries to support the aging populations left behind. Western Europe would find it much easier to manage this challenge if it adopted more liberal policies on immigration, but this is highly unlikely.

Much of the continent already faces significant difficulties in absorbing its existing immigrant population. Many European countries have yet to figure out how to integrate this potentially valuable pool of young people into the economic and social mainstream. Another barrier to growth is that European workers seem content to have traded competitiveness for comfort and security. Economists continue to debate the reason for these differing work ethics. Some argue that high European taxes over the past several decades have created disincentives. More convincing are the economic analyses that pin most of the blame on restrictive labour rules.

Debilitating as these factors may be, the most serious challenge confronting the economies of Western Europe lies still deeper – in the basic model of capitalism that they have embraced. Much like the United States in the first two decades after the Second World War – when what was good for General Motors was said to be good for the rest of the country – today's Western European economy is dominated by large firms. These firms were crucial to Europe's recovery after the war, but today they are holding the continent back. Economies dependent on such behemoths eventually slow down. The US experienced this sort of malaise in the 1970s and early 1980s until a wave of entrepreneurial innovation – centred on the personal computer and later the internet – helped to transform the economy. Companies that did not exist 30 years ago – Microsoft, Cisco, eBay, Google, Amazon – helped to accomplish the revolution. But in Europe this kind of entrepreneurialism is absent. To be sure, some large European firms – Nokia, to take a prime example – have come up with radically new and exciting products or ways of doing business. But the American experience shows that the most reliable source of such change is new, vibrant firms that do not have a vested interest in preserving existing markets.

Why does Europe have such a hard time generating new Nokias? It certainly does not lack brains. Europeans are generally well educated (better educated, arguably, than Americans); yet much of the problem lies in employment regulations that make it difficult for firms above a certain size, typically ten to 50 employees, depending on the country, to lay off redundant or underperforming employees. Although defended as a way of 'saving jobs', these protections ironically have the opposite effect: if firms cannot shed workers in response to market conditions, they will be reluctant to hire new workers in the first place. These difficulties help to explain why the few highly successful new European ventures like Skype, which pioneered internet-based telephone calls, sell out (to eBay, in Skype's case) rather than expand internally. It may also help to explain why would-be European entrepreneurs, like the Paris-born Pierre Omidyar, one of the founders of eBay, move abroad to start their companies, rather than building them in their home countries.

Europe's leaders are aware of these structural problems and have tried to address them. Advocates of radical economic reform for Europe typically urge that the various components of liberalisation be adopted simultaneously, like the 'shock therapy' adopted by several former Soviet-bloc countries after the fall of the Berlin Wall. But such a strategy would be a political non-starter in Western Europe. Instead, at a meeting in Portugal in 2000, they announced the 'Lisbon Agenda' for fundamentally reforming European economies, with the goal of making the EU into the 'most competitive and dynamic knowledge-based economy in the world'. Many of the items on their laundry list of recommendations – reducing the cost of registering new companies, teaching entrepreneurship in technical schools and universities, expanding small-business loans – were intended to promote the creation of vigorous new enterprises. And by European standards, the Lisbon Agenda was radical, but it fell far short of what many observers have been advocating for years. Martin Baily, the former chairman of President Clinton's Council of Economic Advisers, and his colleagues at the Peterson Institute for International Economics, have outlined a series of much more ambitious reforms for Europe, aimed at boosting productivity, making labour markets more flexible, and giving governments greater latitude in fiscal and monetary policy during downturns. Such measures go far beyond anything the European Council or EU member states have envisioned.

None of this is to say that they are starting with a blank slate in Europe. Even though the continent as a whole remains handicapped in many ways, there are 'hot spots' worth noting. The leading example is Ireland, which only 30 years ago was looked down on as the 'poor cousin' of Europe, and now boasts one of the highest standards of living in the world. Lacking the burden of a costly social safety net, Ireland was able to launch its magical economic ride on the strength of a low corporate tax rate, heavy investment in education, and an 'open door' policy for foreign direct investment, along with, it should be noted, some very large temporary subsidies from the EU.

Another European success story can be found in Estonia, which has used its Soviet-era scientific expertise and well-educated workforce to become a leading centre of information technology and biological sciences. Wales, too, is an economic success-in-the-making. Once dominated by coal mining, it has become a force in the European aerospace industry. Indeed, on a larger scale, the whole of the United Kingdom has been able to depart from the continental norm, thanks to privatisation, looser labour rules, and a strong commitment, under Tony Blair's 'third way', to market economics. The results can be seen in the numbers. From 1990 to 2004, per-capita output actually grew a bit faster in the UK than in the US – a fact that did not go unnoticed in the rest of the world. In 2006, the UK raked in $170 billion in foreign direct investment, putting it close behind the US even though its population is roughly one-fifth the size of our own.[3]

As for the rest of Europe, some of the best prospects for serious economic reform can be found in the lower- and medium-income countries, like Spain, Romania and Poland, which feel a strong need to catch up to the living standards of the continental core. If reform proceeds faster on the fringe, a sense of rivalry – and envy – may help to shake France, Germany and Italy into adopting more radical measures.

Any reform package with a chance of success in these economies will have to do its work at the margins. Under the current regime, when firms grow beyond a certain threshold number of employees, they become subject to a panoply of additional regulations, and thus have strong incentives to remain small. The way to address this 'notch' problem, as economists call it, is to allow new firms formed after a certain date to operate under liberalised labour rules and perhaps a lighter regulatory burden in other areas as well. Additional incentives for new-business formation might also be considered, like lowering income-tax rates for some initial period. If Western Europeans need a model for such an incremental programme, there is an obvious one: China. Rather than administering the 'shock therapy' of privatising state-owned enterprises all at once, as happened in post-Soviet Russia and Eastern Europe, China by and large left them alone, while allowing new firms to form and grow. Although this strategy was not, of course, the only contributing factor, the result has been two decades of astonishing growth.

A 'new deal for new firms' would not be a silver bullet for Europe's lethargic economies. But, in combination with other proposals now on the table, like streamlining rules for business registration and teaching the value of entrepreneurialism, the total package could begin to change the way Europeans think. A mindset change might even encourage more of them to see their futures in creating new, high-growth businesses of their own rather than in working for someone else for a lifetime.

Would a set of reforms targeted only at encouraging the formation of new firms stand a chance politically? Could it overcome the ingrained cultural habits and economic expectations of the continent? Perhaps not. If the critics and proponents of such measures agree on one thing, it is that the ultimate goal of reform is the dismantling of the rules and privileges that have defined European economic life for decades. This, however, is precisely what Europeans, especially the parents of children who cannot find jobs in today's rigid system, should want. Indeed, young people themselves are the obvious potential beneficiaries of more dynamic economies. Whether such far-sightedness can prevail in the streets of Berlin and Paris, and in the bureaucratic enclaves of Brussels, is the great open question. Europe has no time to waste.

Carl J Schramm is president and chief executive officer of the Ewing Marion Kauffman Foundation. Robert Litan is vice president of Research and Policy at the Kauffman Foundation.

Viewpoint
Kulveer Taggar, Auctomatic.com

I headed to Silicon Valley in California after graduating from Oxford and working as an investment banker. I'm also a joint founder of the first online student marketplace in the UK, Boso.com, which has members from over 100 universities, has recently received angel funding and was the subject of a Channel 4 documentary. Now, I am currently developing Auctomatic.com, which simplifies selling on eBay.

The future face of enterprise will be defined by those who are willing to take risks, experiment vigorously, and continue in the face of failure. For those wishing to support us, it's important to create an environment that does not punish failure harshly, that supports risk-taking and doesn't look down on people who seek to experiment with new ideas and processes. Environments that can encourage enterprising behaviours will survive change.

Silicon Valley is the model of a risk-taking environment. In London, graduates are much more likely to become consultants, bankers or lawyers and wear their jobs as badges of honour, than risk becoming an entrepreneur and doing something different to their peer group. In Silicon Valley this is the other way round – there is pride in taking a risk and trying to build something for yourself. The environment cultivates collaboration and co-operation. People are very willing to talk or generally help, and 'networking' isn't something that has to be organised or encouraged – it just happens. In my experience this friendly, optimistic and ambitious vibe rewards big thinking, which is sometimes frowned on in London.

One thing I love about the Valley is the speed with which things happen. Ideas develop quickly, leads are swiftly chased up, and typically everything seems to be very fast paced. The consequence is that ideas are quickly tested or iterated on, which weeds out the bad ideas to the net benefit of the economy and wider society. Having good access to risk capital without onerous conditions also encourages this. I've witnessed this first hand in America, whereas I've found the risk appetite among British investors to be low.

If the UK would like to keep people like me from leaving for more enterprise-friendly locations, the entrepreneurial environment must be improved. Based on my own experience of building a start-up, I think new graduates should be given some incentives to join start-ups. It's very hard to compete for talent with big firms that can offer security and a big salary.

One solution would be to tax stock options less heavily so that start-ups can reward early joiners for the risk they are taking. In addition, enterprise curricula should prepare people for the practical aspects of starting a business as this will encourage them to make the leap and get started in the world of business.

Notes

1   L Thurow, *Head to Head: The coming economic battle among Japan, Europe, and America* (New York: Warner Books, 1993).

2   Eurochambres, 'Progress within EU but global comparisons underline need for vigilance', Eurochambres, Brussels, 2007. See www.eurochambres.eu (accessed 17 Jun 2008).

3   UK Trade and Investment, 'Foreign investors continue to favour UK over other European markets', UKTI, 13 Jun 2008.

SECTION 2: THE BUSINESS OF SOCIAL CHANGE

Society's biggest challenges such as climate change and the ever-present issues of poverty are crying out for entrepreneurial solutions. How will changing motivations shape a generation of entrepreneurs and businesses with some of the answers?

Viewpoint
Ronald Cohen, chairman, Bridges Ventures and The
Portland Trust[1]

Social mission is becoming a leading aspect of our age's business culture. It is increasingly a part of how successful entrepreneurs conduct themselves in the world. Entrepreneurs, especially if they have already been successful, are often attracted to the upside inherent in uncertain situations. It is in their blood. Many today are choosing to put something back into society by becoming social entrepreneurs.

Just as we in the private equity industry have climbed a mountain with regard to European attitudes towards entrepreneurship over the last 30 years, I think we as social entrepreneurs can climb a mountain in terms of the perceived risks and challenges of social investment. By bringing in private sector norms of management and efficiency, we can attract private sector levels of management talent into the voluntary sector and, with the help of appropriate tax incentives, we can attract significant investment through the capital markets.

I am not saying we can solve all the problems of society in this way, but I am saying that, by backing social entrepreneurs, we can have the same sort of impact on social issues that private equity has had on the main stream economy.

Social investment is going to be a new asset class. I am sure of it. Ten years from now, people will be saying that pension funds, insurance companies and corporations must allocate a certain percentage of their assets to organisations that provide a social as well as a financial return.

Why are prominent entrepreneurs and others picking up issues that governments used to address and applying private sector business practices to them? Why does Bill Gates decide to leave his business at the age of 50 to devote the next ten years of his life to solving health and social problems? Because he has the confidence he can do it. He built one of the top five companies in the world before the age of 50. Having done that, he believes that he can apply his entrepreneurial mind to solving problems such as AIDS. Why is Warren Buffett backing him? Buffett knows that it is not the money that counts.

Governments have plenty of money. What counts is the entrepreneurial mindset and skill. We are at a sea change where social investment is concerned. Obligation is not a one-way street: politicians and the major financial institutions have a responsibility also to support and foster enterprise, not just for the sake of the entrepreneurs but for the sake of society as a whole. Enterprise is a huge social force.

Notes

1   This viewpoint is extracted from R Cohen, *The Second Bounce of the Ball* (London: Weidenfeld & Nicolson, 2007).

4 Entrepreneurial solutions to insoluble problems

John Elkington

The world is changing, and with it, markets, alongside the core challenges for public policy makers. Incumbent companies are struggling to respond effectively to the new order, opening out enormous opportunity spaces for new types of entrepreneurs. With a new wave of creative destruction, corporate strategies are beginning to shift from their 1.0 variants (focused on compliance) and 2.0 successors (that emphasise citizenship) to much more powerful 3.0 thinking. This wave develops the capacity of leading companies not only to respond to such changes but also to help drive them. Still, the scale of the relevant challenges continues to outrun our collective capacity to deliver. That gap will eventually be closed – the key question is by whom and at what cost?

Entrepreneurs – both in the private and public sectors – will play central roles. Of course, entrepreneurship has been enjoying a pretty extended honeymoon period, stretching back, in the latest cycle, at least to the days of Margaret Thatcher and Ronald Reagan. Although periodic onsets of irrational exuberance have inevitably tarnished some entrepreneurial halos, both the public and private sectors continue to call for better environments to promote the deployment of entrepreneurial solutions. And into this landscape a new set of entrepreneurs is erupting, focusing on a wide range of social and environmental challenges that some people cluster under the heading of sustainable development.

This process is being accelerated as a growing array of socio-economic, environmental and governance dilemmas press in on mainstream decision makers. These include challenges such as climate change, the risk of global pandemics, the growing threat to natural resources like water and fisheries, and the ever-present issues of poverty, hunger and disease.[1] At a time when such prospects seem to narrow and darken our horizons, talented entrepreneurs are creating a wealth of new opportunities. For all of us to benefit into the long run, we must ensure real opportunity for a much greater proportion of the global population. Recent work by SustainAbility attempts to assess the current state of social and environmental entrepreneurship. While an overemphasis on definitions can be distracting, general working explanations of the terms can help us better identify these pioneers.

Social entrepreneurs are entrepreneurs whose new ventures (social enterprises) prioritise social returns on investment. These people aspire to achieve higher leverage than conventional philanthropy and non-governmental organisations (NGOs), often aiming to transform the systems whose dysfunctions help create major socio-economic, environmental and political problems.

By contrast, environmental entrepreneurs may be interested in social objectives, but their main focus is environmental. Some commentators consider environmental entrepreneurship to be a subset of social entrepreneurship, but they are distinct. A major rebranding of the environmental technology sector began in 2002, as the 'cleantech' sector. The Cleantech Venture Network (CVN) defines cleantech as embracing 'a diverse range of products, services and processes that are inherently designed to provide superior performance at lower costs, greatly reduce or eliminate environmental impacts and improve the quality of life'. CVN includes the following sectors: energy generation, storage, infrastructure and efficiency; transportation and logistics; water purification and management; air quality; materials and nanotechnology; manufacturing; agriculture and nutrition; materials recovery and recycling; environmental IT and enabling technologies.

Both social and environmental entrepreneurship address market failures, though the former tends to address failures that are endemic and deep-seated, while the latter increasingly targets opportunities that are closer to market. Strikingly, after a decades-long period of adaptation, at least some of our great environmental challenges are now seen as potentially soluble through the use of new business models and technologies. Our focus is on the possibilities presented by the new societal mindsets, the hurdles entrepreneurs face in scaling their organisations, and the opportunities for greater collaboration with mainstream corporations, government and others.

Social entrepreneurship is emerging as a powerful catalyst of the sort of change that governments and business are increasingly committed to – but rarely know how to deliver. And through these new firms the potential for holistic, breakthrough solutions is considerable and growing. Among the routes to scale discussed by our respondents, the following surfaced repeatedly:

1 grow individual social enterprises
2 establish multiple enterprises
3 get big organisations – whether companies, public agencies or NGOs – to adopt the relevant models and approaches
4 spur public policy legislation designed to fix market failures

Although to keep us grounded, we should point out that while the field may be growing, it remains relatively small. To put rough numbers on the three areas of social enterprise, cleantech and philanthropy, we estimate that less than $200 million is going into social enterprise worldwide from dedicated foundations each year, compared with over $2 billion into cleantech in the USA and EU, and well over $200 billion into philanthropy in the USA alone.

Even with these impressive numbers, money remains the main headache. Accessing capital is the number one challenge for the entrepreneurs we surveyed, with almost three-quarters (72 per cent) putting this at the top of their priority list. Foundations are still the favourite source of funding for social entrepreneurs (mentioned by 74 per cent of respondents), but there is a wider recognition of the need to diversify funding sources. Turning this goal into an action plan, many entrepreneurs believe this financial self-sufficiency is a real prospect within five years. The proportion of respondents expecting to fund their own operations over the same timescale, with little or no dependence on grants, jumped from 8 per cent currently to 28 per cent.

With the need for new funding, there is a real appetite to partner with business. Social and cleantech entrepreneurs are equally interested in developing partnerships with business, but each has different expectations. Social entrepreneurs, in particular, are acutely aware that they often lack the experience and skills needed. A constant refrain was the growing need for brokering between the entrepreneurs and potential business partners.

Locking into a particular view of entrepreneurship could cause us to miss the breadth of effort. For example, it's easy to get excited about small start-ups in the renewable energy field, but we should remember the huge contributions already being made by much larger companies like Acciona based in Spain, Vestas in Denmark or GE in the USA. And there is also a need to focus on ways of supporting social *intrapreneurs*, the change agents working inside major corporations and financial institutions.

But, business can only go so far alone, for real system change we must focus on government. Governments need to do more to shape public policy, public sector targets and wider incentives – for example in relation to tax breaks for the funding of social enterprise.

Fields on a roll tend to become less exciting over time and interest can shift elsewhere. However, the growing importance of the challenges these entrepreneurs are trying to address guarantees that even if there are upturns and downturns in their fortunes, the underlying growth trajectory will be strongly upward. Their clear interest in working with mainstream business and financial institutions distinguishes them sharply from many conventional NGOs, and their capacity to create and deliver real-world solutions makes them significantly more interesting to business. On the government front, a fair proportion of the leading social entrepreneurs have already worked to shape public policy to favour and support their new approaches, with varying degrees of success.

Growing interest in entrepreneurship

Wherever we look, we see growing interest among business
leaders in what social entrepreneurs are doing. Several factors
seem to be central in driving this trend. They also contribute
to the blurring of the responsibilities between public and
private realms.

First, 20 years after the Brundtland Commission put
sustainable development onto the political agenda,[2] a number
of major challenges once seen to be (and often dismissed as)
the preserve of activist NGOs and wider civil society have
pushed forcefully into the political and business mainstream.
This process is often reinforced by the withdrawal or weakening
of government activity. Successive summit meetings of the World
Economic Forum, for example, have focused on an increasingly
interconnected agenda linking such issues as poverty, hunger,
pandemic risks, terrorism, human rights, energy security and the
growing threat of climate destabilisation.

Second, despite the huge progress achieved in corporate
citizenship and corporate social responsibility (CSR) over the
past 10–15 years, there is a growing concern that we may be
reaching the 'limits of CSR'. The December 2006 *Harvard
Business Review* neatly captured this mood with a twinned pair of
articles by Michael Porter and Mark Kramer[3] and Clayton
Christensen et al.[4] The conclusion: too many companies have
seen the new, interconnected agenda as remote from their core
business interests. The reality is that these complex issues pose
increasingly strategic choices that need to be addressed in
suitably radical and higher-leverage ways. This is something that
most corporate citizenship departments seem ill-equipped to do.
But the pressures are clear, as in Wal-Mart's announcement that
it will impose new climate footprint specifications and
requirements on its 61,000 suppliers. This is one more indication
that changes can come from private sector initiative far faster
than when government and public policy channels are attempted
and, often, blocked by effective corporate lobbying.

Third, a number of major corporations have begun to re-
bundle existing activities, and in some cases launch new ones,
designed to meet sustainability-related needs. A case in point has
been GE, with its 'ecomagination' initiative. To illustrate the

scale at which such companies can drive change, if minded to do so, look at GE as an example. When the company released its 2006 ecomagination report,[5] it revealed that revenues from the sale of energy-efficient and environmentally advanced products and services had doubled from $6 billion to $12 billion, with orders in the pipeline jumping from $17 billion to $50 billion. The key point here is that markets are changing and that new offerings are going to be required urgently. Companies that unleash the talents of their intrapreneurs – and form alliances with leading external social and environmental entrepreneurs – will be better placed to succeed.

Fourth, we have seen the emergence of two separate movements that have helped push entrepreneurial solutions further into the spotlight. First, the social enterprise sector has been building for decades, but has been given a major boost by the work of Ashoka and initiatives launched by The Schwab Foundation, The Skoll Foundation, Acumen, Endeavor and *Fast Company* (particularly its Social Capitalist Awards) and many others across the world. Second, the 'cleantech' sector, in part a rebranding of environmental and energy-related enterprise, has seen rapid growth thanks to growing concerns around energy security and climate change – and the recent shift at least in the rhetoric of leading US politicians around issues like climate change.[6]

Time to think differently

To have any chance of changing the world, entrepreneurial solutions must offer relatively high leverage, replicability and scale, and, fundamentally, become part of the market mainstream. Pretty much without exception, the social entrepreneurs we have interviewed are supportive of the idea of partnerships with corporations. They are interested to further develop those partnerships they already had, and to build new ones. This potentially transforms the landscape, shifting the debate from the old forced choice between giant companies that struggle to connect and act, or much smaller niche companies that struggle to reach meaningful scale. In the process, the rise of very different forms of business-to-business and peer-to-peer cooperation holds out real promise of advancing our collective response to very different levels.

The business case for corporate responsibility and sustainability is ever evolving, but always pertinent. The biggest reason that business needs to engage is, bluntly, that the world is changing – and with it so are markets. Social and environmental entrepreneurs do not have all the answers, but they do see the world and markets differently. The innovators are experimenting with new business models that could potentially break out of their niches and help transform key elements of the global economy.

Just as software morphs through successive generations, 1.0, 2.0 and so on, we conclude that the time has come for what we call 3.0 thinking in relation to sustainability challenges. If 1.0 was driven by regulators and promoted a compliance mindset in business, 2.0 has been more about corporate citizenship based on transparency, accountability and a growing array of voluntary initiatives. By contrast, 3.0 thinking, strategy and ventures are different, in that this wave seeks transformative market and sustainability outcomes.[7] It is about creative destruction, as Joseph Schumpeter called it,[8] and about creative reconstruction.

In essence, Mindset 3.0 is about seeing, or 're-perceiving',[9] immense challenges. For example, with the growing risk of abrupt climate changes come potential opportunities to leverage the power of markets and business to reboot entire economic and political systems. This is exactly what is beginning to happen in the energy field. In some cases the time scales involved may be generational, but the transformation is clearly under way. While the cleantech landscape is now largely populated with pure-play profit seekers, the industry was pioneered by individuals who saw the opportunity to leverage market drivers, such as energy security, stability and cost, to realise significant environmental outcomes.

There are a multitude of potential benefits to any company partner working with high performance social and environmental entrepreneurs. Among them is the outsourcing of risk. Companies can minimise potential brand risks, while remaining close to emerging trends by outsourcing research into sensitive or unfamiliar areas such as pharmaceuticals for emerging markets, new energy alternatives, or enhanced foods. They may also be able to bypass strict internal controls around return on investment criteria that would prevent the company investing internally in high-risk, entrepreneurial ventures.

Social and environmental business partnerships can provide access to information, markets and networks. Many social entrepreneurs are working with populations and communities that are unfamiliar to large corporations. It's true that people like Vandana Shiva would no doubt shudder at the idea of opening up wider links between corporations and such grassroots ventures – and for good reason. We certainly should remain acutely nervous about such initiatives being driven in the interests of companies like Coca-Cola or Nestlé. However, with the right caution and balance, the scaling and effective replication of successful solutions can gain dramatically from the resources of the big battalions. The key challenge here will be to select corporate partners strategically, and then to manage the resulting partnerships to hold them true to the small organisation's founding values.

The interests of the potential partners often coincide in various ways. For example, many entrepreneurs have an interest in helping build markets for affordable and accessible mainstream products. On the corporate side, collaboration offers companies access to information about potential consumers and partners and, in many cases, lends additional credibility. It can also spread inspiration. Collaboration with social and environmental entrepreneurs can help companies to tap and recharge their own entrepreneurial and creative spirits, resulting in innovative new product development, eg microinsurance or 'green' products. Consumer goods companies, such as Nike and Marks & Spencer, are beginning to look to social entrepreneurs as a source of originality and competitive advantage for turning out new products.

Those who have worked in this field for some time are excited by the pace of developments at the interface between business and social enterprise. 'The sleeping giant is awakening', says Sara Olsen of Social Venture Technology Group.[10] 'The potential for cross fertilization between social enterprise and mainstream corporations is huge – it's utterly revolutionary!'[11] All true, but for all of this to survive and thrive, the new mindsets, the new business models and the new technologies and tools will have to find traction in markets as they are today. Over time, as the entrepreneurs learn how to work with the more thoughtful big companies, they can begin to lobby more effectively for governments to shape markets to favour these new approaches.

Clearly, all of this needs to come with a powerful public health warning. While our survey revealed willingness on the part of social entrepreneurs to engage corporations, it also highlighted concerns about the potential for mission creep, brand erosion and power imbalances. The implications of these impending shifts are substantial for the NGOs who have done most of the work to date; the companies that have begun to adapt their operations to the relevant challenges in compliance and citizenship; the entrepreneurs who will need to work out how to deliver across the value spectrum; and public policy makers who will need to work out how to shape markets towards more sustainable, more just outcomes.

Feedback from the more seasoned entrepreneurs in our sample offered insights into what would make some of these new partnerships work. A number of them echoed the advice of more traditional NGOs,[12] noting that partnerships work best when there is a clear set of principles and expectations guiding the partnership, eg we only work on projects related to our mission, we respect commercial confidentiality, we understand our business partner's need to pursue ventures that allow them to make a profit. They also stressed that the entrepreneur and partner must have comparable levels of interest in the partnership.

Longer-term partnerships are typically preferred, with social entrepreneurs seeing their organisations and the environments in which they operate as complex, requiring time for an outsider to learn. Cleantech companies, in particular, want to bring in corporate partners early to ensure later options for potential acquisition, what they describe as a 'locked-in exit strategy'.

The role of internal champions in partner companies is cited as essential to building good partnerships. When being acquired by Danone, the French food company's CEO, Franck Riboud was just such a champion for Gary Hirshberg of Stonyfield Farm. Clearly, however, this approach poses real dangers when the individual moves or leaves. Even with engagements that occur at the senior management/corporate level, there are concerns about partners pulling out, indicating a need for entrepreneurs to be adaptable, have a Plan B, and avoid relying on any one individual or department for support.

Overall, our conclusion is that the optimism about these new entrepreneurs is well placed, but that they are experiencing a range of growing pains, and there is an urgent need to steer more capital and business resources into this area. If this can be achieved, we very much agree with Tim Freundlich, director, strategic initiatives, Calvert Social Investment Foundation, and founding principal of Good Capital, that the outlook is bright. 'I see the social enterprise landscape rapidly prototyping strategies that corporations will incorporate; replicate – or just plain steal. These entrepreneurs act as fearless and fast actualisers, taking the uncertainty and lack of imagination out of the equation for mainstream business.'

Business 3.0 will be business as unusual, as the late Anita Roddick put it, and it will involve a radical new set of natural selection processes operating on value chains, business models, companies, industry sectors and, in the ultimate analysis, entire economies. But at the end of this historic reordering of value creation, we will have found solutions that address many – though certainly not all – of the great social and environmental problems that today seem to be impenetrable.

John Elkington is co-founder and chief entrepreneur at SustainAbility.

Viewpoint
Jeremy Leggett, CEO of Solarcentury

As the chief executive of Solarcentury, the UK's largest solar solutions company, I also chair SolarAid, a charity set up by Solarcentury. I've worked both in the oil industry and in the environment movement over the years, and now I am a director of the world's first private equity fund for renewable energy, Bank Sarasin's New Energies Invest AG.

I believe we are in a passage of history that resembles the late 1930s, when we had to mobilise all of a sudden for war. This time the war isn't about the struggle with fascism. This time it is about… us. We humans and the mindless way we use energy. We are on the eve of a hurricane, as the result of our past addictions, and our profligacy. A premature topping point in global oil production would wipe out most if not all plans on offer from corporations, finance ministries and related organisations across the global economy. This is because such plans universally assume growing supplies of generally affordable oil for decades to come. But a surprised world will instead soon be facing rapidly falling supplies of increasingly unaffordable oil.

Warnings by oil industry insiders have recently reached a new pitch that should be sounding alarm bells in every capital in the world. As former US Energy Secretary James Schlesinger has put it, 'we can't continue to make supply meet demand much longer. It's no longer the case that we have a few voices crying in the wilderness. The battle is over. The peakists have won.'[13]

Growing calls for action like Schlesinger's flag the trend that will dominate entrepreneurship and enterprise culture in the UK in years to come. We need this culture to engineer us out of the mother of all global energy crises. This story will not be confined to problems with running our cars or lighting our homes. Everything we do relies on access to safe, clean, conflict-free energy; it is what our civilisation is built on. And though the warnings are obvious, there is barely a register on the radar screen. Politicians almost everywhere, and the vast majority in the civil service and industry, remain locked in an increasingly breathtaking process of institutionalised denial.

This is an issue that needs a Churchill: a leader to warn about the coming clouds, to win the hearts and minds of the British as the threat becomes ever clearer, and make history by leading the mobilisation to survive it. Moreover, it needs all of us ready to work and dedicated to serving the cause, even making sacrifices.

You bet this is a call to arms. We should absolutely be conducting ourselves as if preparing for war. The scale, significance and complexity of the environmental and social issues we will be facing have yet to be accepted. If companies, and the rest of us, are to survive and thrive in the next few decades we need to engage in a real way with the issues now. Once we do mobilise – and we will – design and innovation will have a lot do with whether global human civilisation can survive the coming storm.

Notes

1   SustainAbility, *Growing Opportunity: Entrepreneurial solutions to insoluble problems* (SustainAbility with Allianz, DuPont and The Skoll Foundation, 2007).

2   *Our Common Future*, Report of the World Commission on Environment and Development 'Brundtland Commission' (Oxford: Oxford University Press, 1987).

3   M Porter and M Kramer, 'Strategy and society: the link between competitive advantage and corporate social responsibility', *Harvard Business Review*, Dec 2006.

4   CM Christensen et al, 'Disruptive innovation for social change', *Harvard Business Review*, Dec 2006.

5   GE, *Ecomagination Report* (GE, 2006), available at http://ge.ecomagination.com/site/index.html (accessed 17 Jun 2008).

6   One of the most notable actors in this sector is the Cleantech Venture Network, www.cleantech.com (accessed 13 Jun 2008).

7   Mindset 1.0 has tended to be driven by necessity and by the pressure to comply with emerging regulations and rules. Mindset 2.0 approaches include enhanced stakeholder engagement, sustainability reporting and cause-related marketing, but typically do not offer the prospect of systemic transformation. By connecting to a company's core business, Mindset 3.0 shifts responses into a different gear.

8   J Schumpeter, *Capitalism, Socialism and Democracy* (New York: Harper Torchbooks, 1942).

9   For more, see the work of scenario planners Pierre Wack and Peter Schwartz.

10 In a survey of 21 leading public companies, Sara Olsen and R Paul Herman analysed performance on sustainability processes, metrics and outcomes to develop an exclusive approach to measuring the human and social impact of businesses (see Y Rosenberg, 'Measured progress', *Fast Company*, Apr 2007). Sara came into SustainAbility to discuss the results in mid 2007.

11 Rosenberg, 'Measured progress'.

12 See SustainAbility, *The 21st Century NGO: In the market for change* (SustainAbility, The UN Global Compact and United Nations Environment Programme, 2003).

13 See J Leggett, 'Going, going, gone', *Sublime Magazine* 7 (2007), see www.sublimemagazine.com/goinggone.htm (accessed 17 Jun 2008).

5   The future is social

Jim Lawn

On the face of it, this chapter could be about business and technology, but in fact, it's about neither. It's about people. Business is changing not because of technology, as many might say, but because society is changing and people are using technology to make that happen. The future face of enterprise will celebrate the technological innovation zeitgeist that enables individuals and businesses to succeed on their own terms, including allowing consumers the power to decide what is worth buying. It's the same force that has brought communities together in an attempt to influence large organisations and governments recently.

As Rushkoff said:

The most successful businesses for the next century will turn out not to have been based on infinitely repeatable Harvard Business School lesson plans, but on a combination of competence and passion. Your career is not your job and your company is not its balance sheet. Your most personal choices are, in fact, your business choices. And your business choices may as well be your civic choices. Commerce, communications, civics and community are all part of the same ecology of interdependent activities and needs.[1]

Social media is an internet platform for this ecology, embedding itself within the humanity of community and within the economics and business practices of commerce. It is a set of social tools that bring our democracies closer to the original Athenian sense of democracy: the participation of all the people. Previously, a small number of people could have a large influence over the masses while the masses themselves had little or no opportunity for control. But now, social media tools have dramatically reduced the barriers to entry for individual and mass engagement resulting in multiple and diverse levels of influence from the masses, the 'long tail' of democracy.

At the same time, social media networks are opening up the distribution and sales channels that allow products in low demand or with low sales volume to collectively make up a market share that can rival or exceed the relatively few current bestsellers and blockbusters. By the same theory we have the 'long tail' economy.[2] Through social media, these two 'long tail' principles can open a space for economic democracy. With a larger plurality, we can predict a growing expectation of ethics reflected in the rise of consumer and regulatory interest in transparency, respect, corporate governance, equality and environment. There is also an emerging trend of business and consumer partnerships. Using social media as a platform, customers are becoming active consumer-citizens and some businesses are absorbing social media and ethics to their core.

Social media: the nexus of humanity, technology and business

Social media is a term used to define a set of interactive tools such as journals and blogs, social network sites, communities and forums. These all share the common characteristics of participation, openness, conversation and connectedness. Technologically, social media exists in three evolutionary states. Stephen Johnston once described this evolution as follows:

> Web 1.0: Brain and Eyes (= Information)
> Web 2.0: Brain, Eyes, Ears, Voice and Heart (= Passion)
> Web 3.0: Brain, Eyes, Ears, Voice, Heart, Arms and Legs (= Freedom)[3]

Web 1.0 represents the web technologies of the 1990s that enabled computers to connect with other computers to allow users to search and consume information globally. Classic web 1.0 examples are eBay, Amazon, Google, Yahoo and Expedia. Web 2.0 represents the social media technologies of our current decade enabling not just computers, but also people, to connect and interact with each other globally. Classic web 2.0 examples are Wikipedia, Facebook, Flickr, YouTube and Skype. We reach web 3.0 when the human network and the computer network come together to interact with human-like attributes such as artificial intelligence, semantics, virtual reality and mobility.

Though some would have web 3.0 not starting until the next decade, emerging web 3.0 prototypes are out there. Google Earth allows people to merge their business in all sorts of different ways with a 3D actual/virtual reality representation of the world, allowing the internet to be more like the real world, and so more intuitive and accessible to more people. On the other hand, Second Life's 3D virtual world is entirely built, owned and populated by its nearly ten million virtual residents from around the globe. The real world becomes virtual and provides people with more choice regarding who they are, how they portray themselves and what they do – including doing business. Second Life residents buy, sell and trade with other residents, resulting in millions of US dollars in monthly transactions.[4]

Social media has been a strategic tool for enterprise since web 1.0, but its relevance has become ever more pertinent as consumers and communities have become increasingly confident and determined to voice their passion and realise their freedom. As Kevin Roberts, chairman of Saatchi and Saatchi, has said: 'The consumer is now in total control. They're going to decide when they buy, what they buy, where they buy, how they buy. They are not cynical, they are completely empowered, and they are autonomous.'[5] Once a business appears online, its goods, services, prices, reputation and ethics can be compared and consumer-rated against anyone else's; shopping aggregators like Moneysupermarket, TripAdvisor and Epinions do this automatically.

When Amazon was first coming on to the scene, there was an amount of concern about bad reviews; however, the reality is that reviews are one of the site's greatest attributes. It displays a true understanding of 'transparency' – the idea that all processes are kept out in the open – generating customer loyalty.[6] For a new business, this means that an established competitor will no longer find it so easy to drive them out of the market by underhand tactics or brute force. On an aggregator site, all businesses are equal; your products can be compared and consumer-rated side by side with the biggest players in the game.

Social media businesses flourish by re-embedding into economics the core habits of humanity: sharing ideas; cooperating to create art, thinking and commerce; vigorous debate and discourse; and the need to find people who might be good friends, allies and lovers. It's what our species has built several civilisations on. This has some key implications for any businessperson trying to engage with social media via the internet.

Social networks and communities

One clear trend in up-and-coming business in the social media era is the ascendance of social network services. These are web-based applications whose core function is to help a person establish and maintain social relationships. The exact nature of the relationship is entirely up to the application or platform being used. MySpace, Facebook and Bebo are among the most popular consumer social networks with tens of millions of active users, and in the case of Facebook, growing at 3 per cent per week. Sites like LinkedIn are held up as typical business examples.

The ultimate value of social networking to businesses is still undefined, but at the very least we know it can provide a platform for a business to support sales pipeline generation through large personal networks. Another possibility is a platform for the customer information and discussion communities that are starting to replace the traditional one-to-one customer/company relationship. While your parents might have added communications, marketing and PR to their business after the product was developed, today, marketing, communications and PR *begin* a business.

Taking the concept of social networks and communities further, 'crowdsourcing' was first coined by Jeff Howe in a June 2006 *Wired Magazine* article[7] to describe the act of taking a task traditionally performed by an employee or contractor, and outsourcing it to an unspecified, large group of people, in the form of an open call. Preliminary benefits of crowdsourcing for new businesses and entrepreneurs appear to be the ability to explore problems at comparatively little cost; payment by results; and connection to a wider range of talent than might otherwise be accessible. Clear examples of how this concept has taken off in the social media era would be Wikipedia and YouTube. Another would be Proctor and Gamble, who post problems on a website called InnoCentive, offering large cash rewards to more than 90,000 'solvers' who make up their network of backyard scientists.

The 'long tail' economy

Anderson argued that products that are in low demand or have low sales volume can collectively make up a market share that rivals or exceeds the relatively few current bestsellers and blockbusters, if the store or distribution channel is large enough. Equally, given access to a sufficiently large and diverse marketplace, the chances of a niche community being able to identify niche products is likely to improve. This means more openings for more businesses to get into the game. The internet has given rise to various, and significant, 'long tail' markets. For the first time ever, social media creates the distribution and sales channel opportunities required to help businesses to tap into these markets successfully. An Amazon employee once described the 'long tail' as follows: 'We sold more books today that didn't sell at all yesterday than we sold today of all the books that did sell yesterday.'[8] Translation: Amazon sells more 'unpopular' (long tail) books than it does 'popular' (bestseller) books.

eBay is an example of a large and diverse online marketplace, with 15 million customers in the UK alone and over 10 million items for sale at any one time; they generate total quarterly revenue in excess of £100 million.[9] eBay accounts for 11 per cent of the total time UK users spend on the internet and over 68,000 traders earn their primary or secondary income from trading on the site. Those sellers, seeking a new route to market, can theoretically achieve overnight access to millions of people. All this advantage and there is only a little up-front capital required to start an eBay business. Top eBay sellers (titanium powersellers) all have monthly turnovers in excess of £95,000.

Understandably, eBay may not be a primary trading block for start-up businesses; it is a good example of large numbers of traders making business success in a 'long tail' market. More practically, eBay also offers new businesses or entrepreneurs the opportunity to research and test a market at virtually no cost, helping them to understand pricing sensitivity in relation to their volume of sales. But don't worry; the real world hasn't disappeared yet! There are still companies with a real-life presence outside the eBay site, and those who provide a service to the eBay marketplace itself. Examples would be: Postal Supplies Direct which keeps eBay's army of sellers in packaging materials; and Auctioning4U which sells goods on eBay on its customers' behalf.

For the entrepreneur, harnessing social media and networking in their business is an automatic win. It provides access to research, consumer trends and the opportunity to engage with diverse communities, customers, stakeholders and collective intelligence on a scale that was previously the sole stronghold of big business and institutions. In this digital era, things have changed. In the 'long tail' culture, scale is no longer the deciding factor of market success; individuals can trade within niche groups and create new markets. Through social media phenomena such as crowdsourcing and aggregators, we can skip the middleman altogether causing the rise of the 'ordinary expert'.[10] Social media causes the death of distance through this disintermediation, or transformation, of the nature of media opinion and aggregated business models. Commerce and communications can take place practically anywhere and anytime. A customer can connect directly with an organisation and their perception of the value of the service will eventually impact share prices.

Human creativity, opinion and socialisation open new potential in the connection between business and society. The power of people to become ever more a part of enterprise points us towards a future of relationships and collaboration. This diverse set of entrepreneurs, commentators, and hobbyists can shape end products and ignite movements. Economic democracy promoted through social media is driving business transparency and accountability, as well as enabling greater efficiency. The success of future entrepreneurs engaging in the social media era will be a story of give and take with society – resulting in commercially strong but also sustainable businesses.

Jim Lawn is the co-founder of Meerkat, a not-for-profit organisation and the co-founder of Polecat Ltd, a not-just-for-profit company providing innovation acceleration support and services for not-just-for-profit start-ups.

Viewpoint
John Bird, founder of The Big Issue

I started life in a London Irish ghetto – full of poverty, aggression and violence. My family was made homeless when I was five years old and they put me in an orphanage at the age of seven. Between then and starting up The Big Issue, *I spent most of my life being dishonest: shoplifting, housebreaking and car stealing. After a spell in Paris, I came back to the UK and started a successful printing business. Seventeen years later we started* The Big Issue.

When I see the huge number of people sending me emails with great ideas for social enterprises, asking me for advice, and when I meet the young entrepreneurs themselves, at events, I know that social enterprise is the up and coming trend in the UK.

People want to buy with a good conscience and savvy entrepreneurs can meet the demand for transparent, eco-friendly products. People want authenticity; they want individuality and they want to be able to express their difference and I think we are seeing a switch towards quality instead of quantity. Slowly, there is a return to more simplicity in our consumption, and more 'home made' products on offer. Restructuring the way the market produces and delivers will open lots of routes into ethical businesses that use socially responsible means.

However, social entrepreneurs are caught in a tricky situation. In a sense, they're just financial entrepreneurs displaced by the fact that it's no longer right or sexy to be greedy. Their drive comes from a desire to make their mark in social change. But, as always, it's a question of demand and supply. Creating a company is simple in the UK. Funding the project is the complicated part. It is a pity if good ideas don't become reality because of funding. I created Big Issue–Big Invest with that in mind. It is led by social entrepreneurs and staffed by social financiers. Big Issue Invest is a social enterprise that is a specialised provider of finance to other social enterprises.

The other side of funding, which must be remembered, is how experimentation like this requires failure. Over the years there have been countless mistakes at The Big Issue *and I celebrate that. If you get it right the first time you will never know how you got it right: success with no cock-ups is impossible. Entrepreneurship should be encouraged and funded with this is mind.*

Notes

1   D Rushkoff, *Get Back in the Box: Innovation from the inside out* (New York: Harper Collins, 2005).

2   C Anderson, 'The long tail', *Wired Magazine*, Oct 2004.

3   S Johnston, 'The obligatory 3.0 post: this time with added Youni-corn', weblog entry, *ThreeDimensionalPeople*, 25 Apr 2007, see www.3dpeople.blogspot.com/2007/04/obligatory-30-post-this-time-with-added.html (accessed 14 Jun 2008).

4   See http://secondlife.com/whatis/ (accessed 17 Jun 2008).

5   Interview with Kevin Roberts, conducted by PBS in 2003.

6   iCrossing, *What is Social Media?*, an ebook from iCrossing
     (formerly Spannerworks, Nov 2007), see
     www.icrossing.co.uk/fileadmin/uploads/eBooks/What_is_social
     _media_Nov_2007.pdf (accessed 14 Jun 2008).

7   J Howe, 'The rise of crowdsourcing', *Wired Magazine*, Jun 2006.

8   See www.thelongtail.com/ (accessed 17 Jun 2008).

9   BusinessZone, 'Is it worth starting an eBay business?',
     BusinessZone, Jul 2007, see www.businesszone.co.uk/cgi-
     bin/item.cgi?id=170334&d=1095&h=1097&f=1096&dateformat=%2
     50%20%25B%20%25Y (accessed 14 Jun 2008).

10   J Kuszewski, *The Knowledge Economy* (London: SustainAbility,
     Feb 2007).

6 Demanding good business

Peter Grigg and Joanne Lacey

A new era of social consciousness has dawned with old associations and ideologies being broken down. A host of people are doing surprising things: Al Gore won the Nobel Peace Prize for his efforts in drawing the world's attention to global warming; the Conservative Party are battling on green issues; supermarkets are leading the way by banning plastic bags. Who would have thought, 20 years ago, that any of this was possible? Consumers are increasingly looking to leaders, brands and businesses to help manage their own impact on society. It is now good business to be a good business, as observed through the successes of organisations such as Cafédirect, Belu, Abel & Cole and Marks & Spencer, to name but a few. The Ethical Purchasing Index (EPI) confirms this and values the total value of the 'ethical sector' at £32.3 billion in the UK and growing. The average household expenditure on ethical goods is now £664 per year, almost double the amount in 2002.[1]

But too often trends in ethical consumerism are used as a barometer for the potential relevance of good business. This might be misleading for two reasons. First, we should not presume that people will act on their stated intentions. One study[2] in 2006 found that nearly nine out of ten of under-30s surveyed stated they would switch from one brand to another, price and quality being equal, if the second brand is associated with a good cause. However, a separate survey of 7,000 young people[3] under 25 found that only 27 per cent overall said that they would be willing to pay more for clothes that were ethically produced. This potential mismatch between beliefs and behaviours is referred to by the Co-op Bank[4] as an 'ethical gap' and may leave young people, in particular, feeling powerless to make a difference given that they have less disposable income. Second, and more broadly, conflating trends in ethical consumerism with changes in business misses the point that consumer purchasing power is not the only way to drive change towards more responsible business practice. People also influence the behaviour of companies and markets from within – either as employees shaping company actions or as entrepreneurs developing new markets. So while young people may be limited in their ability to shift corporate behaviour through spending power, it is possible that the desire from young people for fair, fulfilling and authentic opportunities to be part of a good business will shape and drive the future face of enterprise.

For many young people, work is not only what they do, but also an important way they communicate their values to the outside world. It is an expression of who they are and a key element of what is described by some marketing authors as 'brand me'.[5] Professor Richard Scase argues that 'talented young people are very aware of how the reputation of the company they work for spills over to their own peer group… at social gatherings, in the bars and clubs, young people assess each other in terms of their jobs and the companies they work for'. The implication in Scase's argument is that young people, increasingly, do not want to be seen to be working for one of the bad guys.[6] Instead, they want to work for a company that not only tells a good story, but also be part of the story.

Business journals and magazines are packed with articles describing how companies need to respond to this in order to attract and retain the best staff in the so-called 'war for talent'. In light of these new realities the terms of debate seem to be maturing from reputations that demonstrate corporate social responsibility (CSR) to actions that display 'good business'. 'Good business' is hard to define but is a term that has long been circulating through the discourse of CSR and social enterprise. Although the three terms are occasionally used interchangeably, good business is distinct. It does not necessarily refer to business with a primarily social purpose (a social enterprise). And some would describe it as different from CSR in that it is concerned with what a business is doing at its core as opposed to what it is doing to address reputational issues (which is how CSR is often regarded – fairly or unfairly depending on perspectives).

In an attempt to understand the essence of 'good business', the psychologist Mihaly Csikszentmihalyi[7] interviewed several dozen exemplary CEOs including Peter Bijur (CEO of Texaco), Michael Markkula (co-founder of Apple Computer), the late Anita Roddick (founder of the Body Shop) and Ted Turner (vice chairman of AOL Time Warner). They all agreed that 'vision' and 'soul' are what attracts loyal employees willing to go above and beyond the call of duty. Csikszentmihalyi concludes that there are three interconnected factors crucial to the operation of a good business: trust; the commitment to fostering the personal growth of employees; and the dedication to creating a product that helps society. In short, modern businesses can motivate employees and customers by contributing to the common good.

This description resonates with what students say they want from work. One 2006 survey[8] of 2,000 final year undergraduates found that over 70 per cent of students said a company's ethical track record is a crucial factor when choosing an employer. Whereas in the 1980s and 1990s, ethical consumer work focused on improving consumer information and instigating boycotting campaigns, companies now want to manage their reputation and behaviour among employees as well as their customers – they want to focus on *motivation*. Ed Mayo, currently chief executive of the National Consumer Council, describes this when he says that 'the field of corporate responsibility is coming of age. And there is no more sure sign of its maturity than the arrival of fairness as a key concern.' He stresses that fairness is important because it uses language that ordinary people understand.[9] Perhaps every day, 'fair' behaviour seems more achievable than notions of ethical action. This view also seems to be borne out by the popularity of polls and awards such as bestcompanies.co.uk, greatplacetowork.co.uk, ftse4good.com, which recognise companies that uphold values such as fairness and respect. The signs are that the rules of unacceptable business behaviour are being set not just by the consumer, but increasingly by employees themselves.

In a world where information is more freely available than ever before and where people demand openness and participation, *authenticity* emerges as a cherished value in the workplace. This is a trend that is well articulated in books such as *Wikinomics* and others.[10] Employees are regarded as the best route to finding out what a company is really like – hence the ever-growing number of whistleblower sites, Facebook groups, activist's blogs and websites, where disgruntled employees can easily name and shame businesses for unethical behaviour. Richard Reed, the founder of Innocent Smoothies, argues that companies need to respond to this new environment by capitalising on 'the advantages of integrity' as a route to employee retention and the creation of a passion-fuelled workspace.[11] Authenticity and integrity, as aspects of good business, were also at the heart of a panel convened to discuss the relationship between graduates and the workplace. Participants on the Orange Make Your Mark Graduate Panel[12] for example were disappointed that companies were not more open about the types of person they generally want to recruit and the types of opportunities that are on offer. Recruitment adverts and exercises were seen to be deceptive, regarded as 'spin'. Panel members had gone as far as seeking alternative careers after graduating and setting up their own companies just to be given the chance to be themselves and express their own creativity within the workplace.

A mismatch between individual and company values around authenticity or fairness can be particularly damaging to companies when it causes employees to question their commitment to their current job. One Business in the Community survey found that three in five employees want to work for a company whose values are consistent with their own.[13] Another study from Common Purpose suggested that 25–35-year-olds may be particularly anxious about this situation and experience a 'quarter-life crisis'– where successful young employees seriously consider leaving pressurised jobs to search for more meaningful and fulfilling work. In the study, nearly nine out of ten (87 per cent) said they are seeking careers that fulfil their potential at work and that add purpose to their lives, yet 59 per cent admit their job doesn't fulfil their wider ambitions. Fifty-seven per cent said that as a result they are currently looking for a new job and over a quarter hoped to change jobs within the year.[14]

As the Graduate Panel indicated, self-employment and entrepreneurship can emerge as a route out of this frustration. The fact that 'fairness' and 'fulfilment' also resonate strongly with these young people may point to the emergence of a new breed of potential entrepreneurs. Research from Shell LiveWIRE and the London School of Economics compared entrepreneurs who started in the 1980s and early 1990s with those who started from the late 1990s onwards.[15] The older entrepreneurs saw being an entrepreneur as an important part of their identity, projecting an image of being affluent, profit-focused, a risk-taker, individualistic, and in possession of guts and ambition. In contrast, for those who became entrepreneurs from the late 1990s onwards being an entrepreneur has come to mean something quite different. Entrepreneurship is not the be-all and end-all of their identity or career. Instead 'new economy entrepreneurs' are concerned primarily with striving towards a set of ideals that they feel are best achieved through entrepreneurship. It is naïve to think that money is no longer a motivation for young entrepreneurs, but the study found that alongside running a successful business, new economy entrepreneurs are also focused on creating dynamic and enjoyable work cultures and lifestyles where they have control over their time and activities. Alongside a reported greater desire for autonomy and enhanced social consciousness, the Shell LiveWIRE/LSE research also found that many are confused about what to do with it. In general and to a greater extent than older entrepreneurs, however, younger entrepreneurs report an ongoing commitment to fairness and the wellbeing of their work colleagues.[16]

Even where young people do not want to set up their own company, they increasingly demand entrepreneurial and creative places to work. An environment and culture in which an individual can learn, develop and contribute to the success of a business is seen as crucial if a company wants to attract, foster and retain young talent. Yet, evidence seems to show that it is not just about the office environment. A recent survey by Orange found that 77 per cent of businesses reported a problem recruiting and retaining enterprising people and that more than half of the businesses believed that 'different challenges' and the 'nature of the work' keep enterprising employees loyal, rather than just financial reward.[17] Research suggests that many young people assume that the ideal environments in which to express their full potential are small companies rather than large ones. Sixty-four per cent of the young people in the study believed they would be more valued in small companies, even though large companies were still seen to offer better financial rewards and prospects.[18]

Leaping ahead for a second, there seem to be huge opportunities for companies, regardless of size, to tap into the entrepreneurial potential of staff to deliver on good business through 'entrepreneurial CSR' initiatives. For instance, companies could give staff the autonomy, opportunity and finance to use their skills to start up a new project that offers a pragmatic solution to some of the major environmental and social issues of our time. Or companies could work in collaboration with existing social enterprises as mentors to help deliver social contracts. There are many ways that economic development in the form of business expertise, contacts and resources could be used to create sustainable initiatives. The benefits to companies would include new business opportunities, un-tapping the enterprise potential of their employees, demonstrating responsible business in a sustainable way, and satisfying the values and motivations of key staff.[19]

As a concept, it is of course possible that the term 'good business' simplifies too many complex arguments. Attitudes towards good business may also be a luxury from what has been a fairly buoyant economy over the past ten years – a recession may change things. A final caveat is that the language of 'good business' may also be problematic; it is a tradition of youth culture to seek things that are 'savvy' or 'defiant' rather than 'worthy'. Nonetheless, good business is in genuine demand. A cultural synergy exists between the values of young people and the changing values of good businesses. The ethical consumer as a force for good does of course also exist, but there is real demand from young people to want to shape the future of business as business professionals and entrepreneurs, rather than just consumers. Employers will have to respond to this in order to compete for the creative, entrepreneurial, passionate employees who will create future markets.

Peter Grigg is principal policy adviser for the Make Your Mark campaign; Joanne Lacey is an independent researcher for JEL research.

Viewpoint
Mel Lambert, former Group HR Director for IVECO Fiat, entrepreneur and consultant

The future face of enterprise is ethical. Corporate social responsibility (CSR) is becoming one of the biggest issues for business success. The repercussions of recent US business scandals are clearly felt by UK plc. Boards of directors will be rigorously controlled to avoid another Enron. There is a strong drive for high business standards and an ethical business image.

Human resources (HR) plays a huge role when it comes to ensuring ethical enterprise. A business can't be run irrespective of what it does to its people. Businesses must take their employees with them if they are to deliver their business strategy. Only when employees are truly involved and committed can a business be transparent and ethical. Of course, employee involvement also fosters innovation — people who are not involved with the company will not be interested in helping it to get ahead. A business doesn't need listeners, it needs participants.

One of the first indicators of a business heading for trouble is high absenteeism. It means employee motivation is low, for whatever reason. Many companies I consult aren't even aware of the absence rates in their business. There is another quick way to tell whether a business is running well. If you talk to the telephone operator, a PA or someone working in customer services and you don't feel that they are interested in you and what you have to say, there is a problem. It invariably means that employees are not involved in ensuring their company is successful.

Employees need to know what the business wants to achieve, what they can do to help the business achieve, and that they will share in its success. There are several ways to get this message across and ensure employee involvement. Setting up an employee council is one of the first tasks on the to-do list for many businesses. Every six months the chief executive should tell the employees what is going on and what role employees are playing in this. Sharing in the company's financial success through, for instance, performance-related pay and company share schemes, and employee networks are key ways of getting employees totally involved.

Many businesses have CSR high on their agenda already. I believe we are getting closer to a tipping point. Business culture is changing. More and more businesses are realising that they cannot deliver their CSR agenda without high-quality HR management. The future of enterprise will see respectful treatment of all involved in the business process, including employees of the business, suppliers and their employees, customers and shareholders.

Notes

1   Co-operative Bank, *The Ethical Consumerism Report 2007* (Manchester: Co-operative Bank, 2007), see www.goodwithmoney.co.uk/images/pdf/ethical_consumer_report_2007.pdf (accessed 12 Jun 2008).

2   Cone 2006 Millennial Cause Study, *Cause Marketing Forum*, 24 Oct 2006. This work was commissioned by Cone, Inc., an agency that develops and executes leading corporate cause initiatives, in cooperation with AMP Insights. See www.causemarketingforum.com/page.asp?ID=473 (accessed 14 Jun 2008).

3   Survey conducted by TNS (World Panel Fashion), cited in www.guardian.co.uk/business/2006/aug/12/ethicalbusiness.ethicalshopping (accessed 17 Jun 2008).

4   Co-operative Bank, *The Ethical Consumerism Report 2007*.

5   See for instance, T Gad and A Rosencreutz, *Managing Brand Me* (London: Financial Times and Prentice Hall, 2002).

6   R Scase, 'How can we be employers of first choice?', see www.richardscase.com (accessed 14 Jun 2008).

7   M Csikszentmihalyi, *Good Business* (New York: Simon & Schuster, 2006).

8   'Planning for a fairer future', *Guardian*, 15 Jul 2006.

9   E Mayo, Foreword in M Forstater and J Oelschaegel, *What Assures Consumers?* (London: Accountability/National Consumer Council Report, Jul 2006), see www.ncc.org.uk/nccpdf/poldocs/ NCC129_what_assures_consumers.pdf (accessed 14 Jun 2008).

10 D Tapscott and AD Williams, *Wikinomics: How mass collaboration changes everything* (London: Penguin Books, 2006). Others include J Gilmore and J Pine, *Authenticity: What consumers really want* (Boston: Harvard Business Review, 2007).

11 British Library event, 'Ethical entrepreneurs: the rise and rise of good business', British Library, London, 2007.

12 See www.makeyourmark.org.uk/campaigns/students/ orange_graduate_panel (accessed 14 Jun 2008).

13 Business in the Community, 'The business case for corporate responsibility', Business in the Community and Fastforward Research, London, 2003.

14 Common Purpose, 'Searching for something: exploring the career traps and ambitions of young people', 2004, see press release at www.commonpurpose.org.uk/home/resources/research/release7. aspx (accessed 17 Jun 2008).

15 D Slater, 'The changing face of UK entrepreneurism', a Shell LiveWIRE and London School of Economics report, available at www.shell-livewire.org/storc/1182423367.128.pdf (accessed 17 Jun 2008).

16 Ibid.

17 See http://news.bbc.co.uk/1/hi/business/7097185.stm (accessed 17 Jun 2008).

18 Businessdynamics and RSA, 'Intrapreneurship and young people', 2002, available at www.businessdynamics.org.uk/ (accessed 17 Jun 2008).

19 For case studies see www.socialenterprisemag.co.uk/upload/ documents/document25.pdf (accessed 14 Jun 2008). It is also likely that those who took up such opportunities for 'entrepreneurial CSR' would correlate strongly with those staff identified as high-achievers and go-getters.

SECTION 3: ENTERPRISE SKILLS AND MINDSETS

Workplaces, schools and communities all have a role in preparing enterprising people.

What are the future skills and mindsets shaping the future face of enterprise?

Viewpoint
Martha Lane Fox, co-founder of lastminute.com and
Lucky Voice Private Karaoke, and founder of Antigone

*I co-founded lastminute.com in 1998, floated the business in
2000, and remained on the board until the company was
purchased by Sabre Holdings in 2005 for £577 million. I also
founded my own charity Antigone and am a trustee of the
charity Reprieve, a patron of CAMFED and the Prisons Video
Trust, and a co-founder of Lucky Voice Private Karaoke.*

*To me, British attitudes towards enterprise have
changed. There seems to be a much healthier acceptance of
risk-taking and innovation than when Brent Hoberman and I
began our exciting journey starting up lastminute.com. I think
great entrepreneurs are self-aware optimists, they believe things
are possible, are prepared to change the world, want to disrupt
current systems and are passionate about what they are
creating. Living in an enterprise culture will stimulate that
sense of possibility no matter where you work.*

*With the advent and increased use of technology, starting
a business is more and more accessible. The opportunity for
businesses to test ideas first, and then decide if they work before
moving on to the next phase, is enormous. This enables
failures, lessons and an improved product in the end. However,
technology has also made vision and speed of execution even
more important as it opens and creates new markets all over
the globe. Now, a UK company faces competition on a wider
scale than ever before. Businesses know the necessity to remain
competitive will continue to make us think big. I think this
trend will continue as we blur the boundaries between
offline/online businesses as well as between countries.*

*The important thing to remember when promoting
entrepreneurship is to support new ideas, be open-minded and
allow people to fail. This should encourage individuals at all
levels in organisations to act on ideas. Not everyone is an
entrepreneur, nor should be! Nonetheless I am sure that there
are hundreds of people never given the opportunity to see
whether they have entrepreneurial potential.*

*In my own case, my amazing education and the
enormous support that I received from my family certainly*

helped build the confidence and contacts needed to make that first leap. Creating an enterprise culture in the UK needs to start at home and at school with the encouragement, mentoring, sponsorship and apprenticeship of young people. If, as a country, we can nurture and support more of these emotions and abilities then I think Britain will become an even more exciting place to live.

7 Thinking inside the box: the new business reality

Gordon Frazer

Much of the debate about new employee skills sets has tended to focus on how individuals themselves can be more innovative within organisations rather than analysing how the organisation itself can utilise the talents of these individuals. How can entrepreneurs within an organisation be encouraged to innovate? How can people think 'outside the box' when they're 'inside the box'?

The central question is how a large organisation deals with entrepreneurs when they are on the inside. How can their innovative potential be absorbed and why are they so important to the success of a business? Gifford Pinchot,[1] the Harvard academic and leading expert on innovation, characterised the answer as one about how an organisation can foster intrapreneurship – people who focus on innovation and creativity within the organisational environment, often taking their inspiration from their founder's example. Importantly, our experience at Microsoft has confirmed that supporting this intrapreneurial behaviour is often the best way of promoting company-wide innovation.

Although some academics examine the structural, cultural and operational issues that corporate entities face in making the most of their entrepreneurial employees, this has yet to trickle down into public discourse and policy discussions. Yet a better understanding of this evolution is important because across UK plc we are faced with a new business reality: one in which networks and relationships are facilitated online and collaboration is the norm. In this new reality people entering the workforce expect a more fluid hierarchy and a greater level of autonomy in how they work. This is the daily routine for new economy companies like Microsoft and it is an essential part of an economy that is increasingly dominated by knowledge: the flow of information that makes a business work and the possession of which helps to facilitate enterprise. For us, innovation is the process of converting a creative idea into a new and tangible product or service that offers significant value to business, government or individuals. This can cut across technical, societal, governmental, organisational and business process lines; it is something new and exceptional that delivers a beneficial outcome. Innovation is fundamental to achieving continued business growth and success.

Employee empowerment that allows intrapreneurial behaviour is the first step in expressing innovation. Chris Adams, one of our graduate trainees in the Information Worker Business Group, recently mentioned to me: 'All the people I work with ask questions about what we're doing, how it's being done and whether it could be done better. We're not afraid to challenge the status quo.' This is hugely exciting for us. We need fresh ideas and fresh ways of looking at our business. It's an attitude that is at the heart of innovation and the core of an enterprising business. It's part of the new reality we all face; a more demanding workforce, a more demanding market and a greater sense of ownership and aspiration from our employees. We welcome this trend, but it also necessitates new operational systems for managing a worldwide organisation.

The vision Chris articulates describes a world where intrapreneurs drive change by asking more questions, being more resourceful and ultimately having more autonomy and ownership in what they do. The challenge of achieving this is something we work through everyday. It's increasingly prevalent for organisations of all sizes to seek to develop this new environment, from small- and medium-sized enterprises (SMEs) and community groups to major multinational corporations and government departments. It is also part of a wider phenomenon built around the knowledge economy. The changing expectations of new recruits mirror a more demanding business environment where global competition compels us all to look at new ways of generating a competitive advantage. The game heats up even more when the increasing number of highly skilled and enterprising graduates from developing economies, such as

China and India, are thrown into the mix. With this backdrop, the ability to stay ahead of the curve, to have new ideas, and create new opportunities has never been more important.

But being known for creative products is only one side of the coin. The other, more critical, factor is providing the infrastructure needed to capture the great ideas that intrapreneurs develop. This is something that many organisations still fail to grasp but which is of great importance in delivering productive innovation. Intrapreneurs, by their very nature, are eager to see change and progress. If their ideas are held back they can quickly become frustrated and disenchanted, and may even vote with their feet and leave. Systems and processes, therefore, need to be in place in order to channel that energy into a meaningful reality.

Organisational and operational innovation

If knowledge workers are more willing to be inventive in their approach, and the knowledge economy demands it, how can businesses make sure their people feel safe enough to fulfil their enterprising potential? How can businesses encourage the intrapreneurship that can occur as part of the job?

The conventional wisdom of recent times has been captured in the three Ds: de-bureaucratise, de-layer and decentralise. But centralised, commanding systems and procedures are among the hallmarks of large organisations; they help deliver the accountability, transparency and efficiency that make a business run effectively. These processes can at times be cumbersome and inhibitive, but they can also be facilitators of intrapreneurship and innovation. Recent research, conducted by knowledge partners at the Centre for Innovation through IT (CIIT), concluded that 'the impact of organisational culture on innovation cannot be overstated. Strong leadership that develops a culture supporting innovation is pivotal. An environment that encourages communications and knowledge-sharing across organisational boundaries is vital.'[2]

As the CIIT research underlines, the nature of an organisation's culture is decisive in creating successful innovation. A culture is delivered by leadership but importantly also by the organisational structures and procedures that are put in place. For instance, for new ideas to flourish, people need to feel uninhibited to challenge an accepted view or way of doing something, to openly collaborate and debate ideas and concepts. One of the ways Microsoft has done this has been through setting up business groups like the Information Worker Greenhouse. The group is a small incubator within the company charged with fostering new products. Ideas are pitched to the group, good ideas are prototyped, and eventually the Greenhouse team looks to commercialise the product.

An example where this process has delivered tangible and marketable innovation is through Knowledge Network for Office SharePoint Server 2007. The whole purpose of this product is facilitating networks in enterprises and organisations by automating the sharing of undocumented knowledge and relationships. The development of this was something of a virtuous circle of innovation; it was a solid product in itself, but is also a tool that helps capture and replicate creativity through greater collaboration and knowledge sharing. The Greenhouse incubator is important because it's an open and transparent process built around an organisational initiative to find space for creative thinking. As we continue to experiment, we realise our own processes of knowledge generation can become products that help others do the same. We are all in this changed world together and the more we share, the better we get.

To stimulate competition and entrepreneurial thinking, we've also implemented a *Dragons' Den*-style internal panel where new ideas can be pitched for funding. In addition, we have an online intranet site called 'My Ideas' through which people can log suggestions about ways to improve the business. These tools are important facilitators and, crucially, they send out a clear message to employees that they should be acting entrepreneurially and challenging established norms.

This type of leadership in an organisation is critical to setting the tone of an experimental culture. At Microsoft, Bill Gates has done a great deal to create a vision for innovation in the business. Two or three times a year, he sets aside dedicated time to think about the future. Ahead of these 'Think Weeks', there is a call for white papers from across the business – an invitation that is open to anyone in the organisation. This initiative is a strong signal that the leadership of the company is listening to ideas and thinking about the big questions and challenges. But more importantly it sends the message that dreaming is not only okay, but highly valued. As much as anything, these types of initiatives speak to people's emotions and provide a sense that employees can achieve great things which can help to inspire and motivate other groups within the business.

Hiring more 'emotionally intelligent' and entrepreneurially minded people does of course bring with it certain challenges in terms of management. Our experience has taught us that these people respond well to flexibility and autonomy but that most importantly they need to feel they are making a real difference – that their ideas and actions are ultimately changing people's lives. John Kotter, the highly influential Harvard Business School professor, has emphasised the significance of speaking to people's feelings to engender change and innovation. He argues how 'not only is an emotional pull more inspiring, it also encourages people to connect and collaborate to problem solve'.[3] Based on this information, we work with the principle of 'management by objectives'. The central belief is that if you give a clear explanation of the 'what', a responsible employee can work out the 'how'. It is not enough to train our managers in this principle; so much of the implementation is also about building a relationship of trust and transparency between colleagues. For instance, MyMicrosoft is a recently introduced intranet tool that gives detailed information about how staff at all levels can manage flexible working by understanding exactly what is expected of them. This is all underpinned by an embedded belief that technology can transform people's lives for the better and that Microsoft has a unique role to play in doing this. This belief helps to keep our 'emotionally intelligent' people motivated.

Getting the most out of intrapreneurs in a business demands a strong business philosophy, but there is also a need to provide an inspiring physical space that sets the stage for creative exchange. At Microsoft we've designed office space that includes Anarchy Areas: informal, fun and playful places designed for employees by employees to encourage networking and idea generation. It also functions as a space where people can go for a break to unwind and recharge. In our experience some of the best ideas are born when one is away from one's desk and these areas are a way of allowing for this.

Sustaining disruption

For businesses, all this effort is a worthless exercise unless it contributes to delivering the bottom line. Business leaders are constantly challenged to balance development investment with delivering immediate business value. This is a conundrum that has been characterised as a conflict between disruptive and sustaining innovations.[4] The brand new products that evolve out of a company's medium- to long-term investment in R&D are different from new, cheaper and simpler products or services brought to market swiftly. Even though they both challenge and frequently transform market assumptions and norms, disruption is a quicker and more intense change.

The assumption is that large companies do not need to be disruptive to be innovative. As long as they empower their people in their day-to-day jobs, improvements will happen organically. We have never subscribed to this belief. Even large companies need to adopt the agility and disruptive approach of smaller organisations to stay competitive; they need to act smaller to be bigger.

To confirm our culture of disruption, we have invested in a centre for innovation and a research lab closely linked to Cambridge University. It's here that some of our most exciting product developments have taken place, such as the Microsoft Surface[TM5] platform. But these initiatives are not only hubs of innovation in themselves, they are also part of a broader strategy to engage with educational institutions and tap into some of the cutting-edge research taking place externally. Our Emerging Business Team provides a similar function, tasked with harbouring start-ups outside the company and helping them succeed through the networks and expertise our business can offer. Reaching out externally is way of injecting fresh thinking and new ideas internally.

Our business is built around the partner ecosystem, including over 30,000 enterprises in the UK working on Microsoft platforms. This is where some of the most exciting conversations are taking place and where we have a great opportunity to support and benefit from it. For instance, in the area of accessibility science, a company called Dolphin Mobile Access has developed a powerful Smart Phone that incorporates speech recognition and other accessibility features. Supporting the R&D taking place in these enterprises is vital to our business; ultimately a healthy and innovative ecosystem creates increased demand for Microsoft services. But more importantly, an open approach also helps our business stay competitive through knowledge-sharing partnerships and information flows.

The Microsoft journey

As Microsoft has grown, it has experienced the same challenges that many large multinational businesses face in the twenty-first century. Growth, both organic and through merger and acquisitions, creates complex communication and decision-making lines which demand an increase in management processes. Balancing this with the need to cultivate the entrepreneurial side of our employees is a tricky line of tension. This is especially true in a business that operates across the world where cultural issues and differing approaches create further challenges.

As a start-up 30 years ago, full of bright-eyed optimism and a sense of being on the cusp of something truly great and transformational, Microsoft embodied many of the characteristics that are commonly associated with a ground-breaking company. Microsoft has grown into one of the most recognisable and influential companies in the world, and although innovation has always been at the heart of what we do, we now face the challenge of maintaining this momentum.

One thing we rarely think about is the internal cultural differences in companies with different national bases. Traditionally, most people assume that America is more entrepreneurial, and Europe is more risk-averse. Our experience, however, has been that countries such as the UK are witnessing more opportunities, and building many more quality companies. The buzz around universities, and the technology-based enterprises that spring out of them, is testament to this. Technology hubs around the Thames Valley, Cambridge and Scotland's 'Silicon Glen', for example, are further demonstrations of the UK's growing capacity to grow successful enterprises out of this activity. In many respects, we can see parallels to the dynamism that we helped to create in Silicon Valley.

As an international company, we need to provide room for connecting ideas across geographical boundaries. The integral role Microsoft's research lab in Cambridge played in the development of Microsoft Surface™ is an example of how our best skills can come together successfully regardless of location. We have made efforts, as we've grown, to foster a global culture of collaboration built on the principle that the best skills in the business should be used to meet the appropriate challenge, rather than operating in silos. Global gatherings, such as the Microsoft TechFest (technical festival), bring together researchers from around the world to learn and share knowledge face-to-face through demonstrations and lectures from the company's leading innovators.

The tools, infrastructure and operational systems must be in place to facilitate innovation, but ultimately these are ineffectual unless you have the right people to hire. As Microsoft has grown over the last 30 years, we have developed recruitment processes around core competencies that mirror our corporate mission. People are hired on the basis of their passion, their creative potential and drive rather than solely their technical aptitude. Furthermore, we don't think of innovation as purely in the domain of the executive suite or business development group. Everyone has a role to play, from call centre and production workers to people in the international executive team. Innovation should be approached in its most lateral sense as a value that permeates all corners of a business.

We believe the future face of enterprise in the UK is a partnership based on imagination. In our experience, one of the most effective ways of endorsing this is by keeping intrapreneurs inside an organisation engaged. At Microsoft we strive to keep alive a passion about the power of technology to change the world. It motivated Bill Gates 30 years ago and it continues to motivate our intrapreneurs today. These people need to feel that they can ask the demanding questions, be creative and action their ideas. Importantly, though, to achieve tangible innovation, people also need to have the channels and systems through which to make their ideas come to life. As Bill Gates once commented: 'Never before in history has innovation offered promise of so much to so many in so short a time.' Our challenge is to make this promise become a reality.

Gordon Frazer is managing director at Microsoft Limited in the UK.

Viewpoint
Kyle Whitehill, director of Enterprise, Vodafone UK

I am director of Vodafone UK's Enterprise Business Unit and a member of the Vodafone UK board. I am also a trustee of the Vodafone UK Foundation and a member of the West Berkshire Education Business Partnership's board of trustees.

Last year I was fortunate enough to be invited to speak at the launch of Enterprise Week. One of my fellow speakers that day was Professor Richard Scase – a top academic and serial predictor of future business scenarios. One of the things that Richard drew my attention to has stuck with me ever since. He said that Bill Gates, who should know a thing or two about this, has proclaimed that while the twentieth century was the age of the global corporation, the twenty-first century will be the century of the SME. Richard, for the record, thinks that Gates is absolutely right. In order to remain competitive, he says, large corporations faced with a new style of flexible, adaptive businesses will have to restructure and continually reinvent themselves.

As the manager of a multimillion pound business unit, employing thousands of staff, it is not difficult to imagine why I find this hypothesis intriguing. We even investigated further and did our own study, which confirmed that the happiest and most prosperous companies in the country were found to be post start-ups with fewer than 50 employees. Based on these findings, my main concern in my position is the future role of the country's biggest businesses. Just what should that role be?

First, I believe that big business should be actively supporting and encouraging start-ups and SMEs, something we have been doing at Vodafone for a number of years now, way above and beyond simply providing them with a mobile phone. It's good for our business, and it's good for the economy as a whole.

Second, with regard to my own organisation, it is clear to me that it is my responsibility to ensure that creativity and entrepreneurial behaviour is able to thrive within the corporate structure. By doing this, my aim is to ensure that when young people come on to the job market, they are still attracted to us.

The twenty-first century won't only be the century of the SME – it will be a war for talent. The career options available to young people will be more varied than ever, and the 'blue chips' will no longer be able to assume that they are the default choice of the brightest and the best. We all need to take heed. At Vodafone, we are preparing already.

Notes

1   G Pinchot, *Intrapreneuring: Why you don't have to leave the corporation to become an entrepreneur* (New York: Harper & Row, 1985).

2   Cited in G Frazer 'How to nurture innovation in your business', *Computer Weekly*, Dec 2007, www.computerweekly.com/Articles/2007/12/06/228478/how-to-nurture-innovation-in-your-business.htm (accessed 18 Jun 2008).

3   J Kotter, *Heart of Change: The real life stories of how people change their organizations* (Boston: Harvard Business School, 2002).

4   C Christensen, *The Innovator's Dilemma* (Boston: Harvard Business School, 1997).

5   Microsoft Surface™ is a revolutionary interface that allows users to grab data and move it between objects using natural gestures and touch.

8 Enterprise and social mobility

Duncan O'Leary and Paul Skidmore

In the halcyon days of the dot.com boom, it was widely assumed that our working lives had taken a distinctly entrepreneurial turn. Inspired by the easy fortunes that seemed to be available, more of us would start our own businesses. Those of us who stayed within organisations would use the new power of the communications revolution to do our jobs in more creative ways. And all of us would have to get used to a world in which the pace of change would be unrelenting: to prosper, we would have to take more responsibility for plotting our own course and investing in our own skills, or risk being caught in the next round of downsizing, outsourcing or restructuring. In short, careers were out; enterprise was in.

But did the turn of the century really mark such a turning point in the world of work? In this chapter we argue: first that career patterns are not changing as much or as quickly as was earlier thought – but that the opportunity to enjoy a secure career is unevenly distributed. Second that enterprise is not yet offering a route out of this problem. Third, that there are some universal elements of economic and social policy that will help both those in waged work and those with ambitions to start an enterprise. And finally, that broadening opportunities for enterprise brings its own specific challenges and will therefore require some particular policy responses.

Uneven access to the things we like about careers

The best current evidence suggests that career patterns are not changing as much or as quickly as was earlier thought. In the early 2000s, surveys did appear to show that job tenure had shortened compared with the mid 1990s.[1] However, analyses using longer time series, as well as cross-national comparisons, paint a different picture. One study of the OECD countries, including the UK, found that there was little or no change in job tenure between 1992 and 2002, and in some countries it actually increased.[2] In their analysis of changes between 1975 and 2000, Paul Gregg and Jonathan Wadsworth found no overall decline in job tenure, although it had fallen for some groups and increased for others.[3]

What does seem to have happened, however, is that access to what was good about careers – stability, progression, skill acquisition – has become more unequal. Those with lower qualifications are more likely to be forced to leave their jobs due to bouts of unemployment and less likely to change jobs out of choice.[4] Furthermore, it remains true that the highly qualified are more likely to update their skills in adult life – people without qualifications are three times less likely to receive job-related training than those with some qualifications.[5] The paradox, in social terms at least, is that the least qualified are also the least likely to take part in formal learning in adult life.

In brief, those with no qualifications get the worst of both worlds: those who can find steady jobs are often unable to turn them into steady careers; others fare even worse, facing precarious employment punctuated by repeated returns to unemployment.

Uneven opportunities to start successful enterprises

Given this instability at the bottom end of the labour market, opportunities to form new enterprises represent an important alternative career path. But the evidence on enterprise also makes clear that some of the dot.com era predictions were somewhat overstated. More people *do* work for themselves than they did a generation ago, with many new businesses being built around new models of working in people's own homes. Between 1984 and 2005, the number of self-employed people increased by 626,000. However, all of this increase occurred in the second half of the 1980s. Indeed, despite a strong upward trend since 2001, self-employment was still lower at the beginning of 2006 than it was in 1989 or 1990.[6] These trends have also occurred against a growth in overall levels of employment: as a proportion of total employment, self-employment remains roughly where it was in 1988 (13.3 per cent).[7]

And, as is the case with waged employment, there are issues of fairness and opportunity to be addressed. The problem, again, is that not everyone has the same chance of becoming an entrepreneur. Just as those with few or no qualifications are unlikely to be in waged work, they are also less likely to become entrepreneurs. A 2007 survey found that 45 per cent of entrepreneurs had a degree, more than three times the average for the working age population as a whole.[8]

The effect of this is that those with poor employment prospects often *also* lack the opportunity to redirect their careers towards enterprise and self-employment. Self-determination, both inside and outside of organisations, is unevenly distributed.

Human capital

In this context, the publication of the Leitch Review of Skills represents an important moment for the UK. The ambitions set out in the review – and adopted by the government[9] – will be important not just for future competitiveness, but also in addressing some long-standing inequalities.

However, the challenge for policy, where enterprise is concerned, is to do two important things: to engage the disengaged in learning *and* to reflect the kind of learning that will drive enterprise. While political will power is there to achieve both of these goals, the risk is that policy is too prescriptive about what can and can't be learnt with public money to achieve them in implementation.

At present, public funding for adult learning revolves around full qualifications that are identified, by sector skills councils, as 'economically valuable'. Policy is structured this way for understandable reasons: qualifications are 'portable' for individuals in the labour market and measurable for government. And it stands to reason that government should want to fund courses that will produce an economic return on social investments.

The question, though, is who is best placed to identify an 'economically valuable' course? And will the 'economically valuable' framework be sufficiently supportive of *new* sources of value in the economy? The logic of a 'demand-led' system is that individuals and businesses are best placed to understand their own needs – and indeed they may be the *only* people who know their own ambitions. A yoga course is economically valuable if you are about to start a yoga business. Trying to predict what might be economically valuable for an individual's future, then, makes the leap that sector skills councils will be able to predict and keep up with fast-moving labour markets *and* be aware of what each individual needs to fulfil his or her ambitions.

The further risk is that the system is overly prescriptive and ends up cramping the innovation that is needed to attract and meet the needs of the most disengaged. Creating new demand – for learning, in this case – is often achieved not just through delivering the same thing better, but through creating new products altogether. It comes not just from meeting existing preferences, but through anticipating new, unarticulated demand. As Mick Fletcher points out, few of us were demanding iPods until they entered the shops.[10]

In other words, government should allow people to make their own choices about what is economically valuable at any one time. Unless this can be achieved, the danger is that the needs of present employers – and the interests of existing learners – will overshadow the needs of new learners, and new entrepreneurs.

This is not to argue that qualifications do not matter, or that governments should have no say in their make-up. Rather it is to suggest that policy should look to specify only a few basic elements in all qualifications rather than seek to prescribe in any great detail. Flexibility and the scope for product innovation are vital if new demand for learning is to be created and the needs of future entrepreneurs are to be met.

Social and financial capital

As more evidence emerges, it also becomes clear that qualifications and learning are only part of the recipe for widening the opportunities available to people. The wide-ranging Equalities Review, commissioned by the government, identified a number of 'employment penalties' in the labour market – highlighting differing outcomes between social groups that persist even when factors such as age, ethnicity and level of educational qualifications are controlled for.[11]

As previous Demos research has inferred, this reveals that equality of opportunity is more than simply an issue of human capital. People with the right skills and attributes still require opportunities to *make use of* those qualities, either inside organisations or through starting their own businesses.[12] Here, two other forms of capital are important: social and financial.

In 1973 Mark Granovetter revealed the importance of personal networks in securing job opportunities,[13] demonstrating that in the labour market 'who you know' genuinely does matter as much or more than 'what you know'. In smaller businesses, where recruitment often takes place informally through networks, this may be especially true – and helps explain the way in which smaller organisations in highly networked sectors tend to replicate themselves over time, producing quite homogenous workforces.[14]

There is good reason to believe that these factors apply to starting successful enterprises: and evidence suggests that individuals starting businesses without adequate social contacts and networks are more likely to fail than those who enjoy these benefits.[15] Indeed, one wide-ranging review of the literature on SMEs and entrepreneurship in low-income communities found that differences in social capital were one important part of the explanation for greater levels of enterprise in wealthier areas.[16]

Furthermore, with the exponential use of social network sites online among young people in particular – 55 per cent of online teenagers have a profile on MySpace or Facebook compared with only 20 per cent of adults – the danger is that the gap between the well connected and the rest is only likely to grow as the web enables 'weak ties' to be maintained ever-more easily.

And with investment opportunities increasingly channelled through networks,[17] access to finance can also be hard to disentangle from the strength, or otherwise, of people's personal connections. This seems particularly important given research findings that failure rates for entrepreneurs from lower-income groups are higher than those for wealthier backgrounds and that individuals from low-income families often start businesses without adequate capital.[18]

The challenge for policy makers

Given the complexity of these issues, what should the response from policy makers be?

Universal elements of policy

There are some generic, or universal elements, of economic and social policy that will apply across waged work and enterprise. Key among these will be enhancing opportunities for people to benefit from education and training, which will ideally lead to more people enjoying greater job security.

The most celebrated approach here is the Danish system that combines investment in skills, active labour market policies and generous unemployment benefits with flexible labour markets. The result is that Danish workers *ought* to feel quite insecure, their worker turnover is about 30 per cent a year, and job tenure is relatively low by international standards – close to the levels in the US and the UK. But Danes actually emerge feeling the most secure and the most satisfied in work among all nationalities studied across the OECD.[19] Security is reconciled with flexibility safeguarded by an active state.

Of course this broad framework still requires learning and welfare policies that are, themselves, flexible and innovative enough to meet the dynamic needs of individuals and organisations. But the broader point stands. The Danish system helps mitigate the risk of unemployment – whether due to a failed entrepreneurial venture or the absence of waged work – through providing security and opportunity for those who might otherwise suffer from the predicament of low-skilled, insecure work.

Enterprise-specific polices and approaches

It is also clear, however, that the broadening opportunities for enterprise bring their own challenges and will require some specific policy responses. Overlaying universal elements of policy will need to be strategies that support wider access to social and financial capital in particular.

Part of this will be achieved by ensuring that people have the capabilities to grasp opportunities to gain new contacts and finance when they come along. Entrepreneurs themselves point to the need for a range of attributes not necessarily captured in traditional qualifications. A healthy attitude to risk and resilience in the face of failure are regarded as the kind of 'entrepreneurial behaviours' likely to lead to success in launching a new business.[20]

Developing these attributes implies a learning curriculum that does more to develop some of the entrepreneurial behaviours and capacities described earlier in this chapter. Scotland's 'Curriculum for Excellence' and some innovative work in Northern Ireland already point the way to a more rounded approach here. But more than this, there is an enabling role to be played, not just in providing people with the right skills, but in helping people *make use of* them. Creating opportunities for networking, peer support, mentoring and work experience are crucial. Sector skills councils should be expected to show leadership here. As sector-wide bodies, they should concentrate on functions that are beyond the reach (or interest) of any one organisation in their sector. This includes focusing on attracting future employees and encouraging potential entrepreneurs in their sectors. Equality goals should be at the heart of their respective remits to help ensure this.

While much of the conventional wisdom about careers and enterprise is off the mark, it is not entirely inaccurate. For the low-skilled at the bottom end of the labour market, such career structures as were available are now close to completely disappearing, while the chances of a starting a successful enterprise are comparatively slim. As we learn more about the determinants of success, it becomes clear where policy can and should be making a contribution.

Enterprise is, by its very nature, something that individuals must make happen for themselves. What public policy can be expected to do, however, is to level the playing field and to ensure that opportunities to participate are spread as widely as possible.

Duncan O'Leary is a senior researcher at Demos and Paul Skidmore is a McConnell Fellow in the MPA program at the Woodrow Wilson School of Public and International Affairs at Princeton.

Viewpoint
Iqbal Wahhab, chief executive, The Glorious Group

I am the chief executive of The Glorious Group, which owns and operates restaurants and bars in London. I also chair the Department for Work and Pensions' Ethnic Minority Advisory Group and sit on the ministerial Ethnic Minority Employment Task Force.

Running my own businesses for the least 15 years has taken me from being a one-man show to heading a team of 250 people. Six years ago I opened an Indian restaurant and nobody batted an eyelid and then two years ago I launched a British restaurant, called Roast. That's when I noticed something very interesting. Although I have spent all but the first eight months of my life in Britain, the media coverage was all about a Bangladeshi doing British food. Suddenly by doing something really British, I wasn't British anymore.

Underlying this reception was the expectation of ethnic minority entrepreneurs to stick to their chosen paths. The future face of enterprise has to be different. Society must embrace diversity in enterprise and not pigeon-hole people with stereotyped expectations.

Similarly, ethnic minority-owned businesses need to integrate themselves more into the society in which they are based. Talk of corporate social responsibility, social enterprise and diversity just wasn't around when I first went into business, and now it is being embraced by big business. Partnerships between local business and community help us push the agenda for change from the ground. When we opened Roast, our company chairman Akbar Asif suggested we donate the profits generated from one table to support the work of The Prince's Trust.

Community Partnerships also work through giving time. I take children from disadvantaged backgrounds out for a food awareness day by taking them around Borough Market where they get to see, invariably for the first time, what food is really about. I then give them tasks in our restaurant to tie into what they learned. We are now planning an apprenticeship scheme for school leavers wishing to work in hospitality.

I want to encourage more businesses to embrace social responsibility in their corporate thinking. We can teach corporate business ethical innovation through the examples that stem from the small and local. These partnerships benefit us all. Knowing how few female or ethnic minority CEOs head big firms and how many head up small firms, maybe we can push change there next.

Notes

1   C Macaulay, 'Job mobility and job tenure in the UK', *Labour Market Trends* 111, no 11 (2003).

2   P Auer, J Berg and I Coulibaly, 'Is a stable workforce good for the economy? Insights into the tenure–productivity– employment relationship', Employment Analysis and Research Unit, Employment Strategy Department, working paper 2004/15, see www.ilo.org/public/english/employment/ strat/download/esp15.pdf (accessed 14 Jun 2008).

3   P Gregg and J Wadsworth, 'Job tenure in Britain 1975–2000. Is a job for life or just for Christmas?', *Oxford Bulletin of Economics and Statistics* 64, no 2 (2002).

4   Macaulay, 'Job mobility and job tenure in the UK'.

5   G Broadbelt, K Oakley and D O'Leary, *Confronting the Skills Paradox: Maximising human potential in a 21st century economy*, a provocation paper (London: Demos, 2007), available at www.demos.co.uk/publications/skillsparadoxprovocation (accessed 14 Jun 2008).

6   See www.statistics.gov.uk/STATBASE/
    Analysis.asp?vlnk=214&More=Y (accessed 14 Jun 2008).

7   Ibid.

8   YouGov poll of 2,427 SME owner-managers from across the UK.
    Fieldwork was undertaken between 11 and 17 May 2007. See
    www.newsroom.barclays.co.uk/Content/Detail.asp?ReleaseID=11
    48&NewsAreaID=2 (accessed 14 Jun 2008); P Bates, *Labour
    Market Overview 2006*, for Institute of Employment Studies, see
    www.employment-studies.co.uk/summary/summary.php?id=429
    (accessed 14 Jun 2008).

9   *World Class Skills: Implementing the Leitch Review of Skills in England*
    (London: Department for Innovation, Universities and Skills,
    2007).

10 M Fletcher, 'Do the brokers know best?', *Adults Learning*,
    NIACE, 2007.

11 *Fairness and Freedom: The final report of the Equalities Review*
    (London: Cabinet Office, 2007), see
    http://archive.cabinetoffice.gov.uk/equalitiesreview/
    (accessed 17 Jun 2008).

12 D O'Leary, *Recruitment 2020: How recruitment is changing and why
    it matters* (London: Demos, 2007).

13 M Granovetter, 'The strength of weak ties', *American Journal of
    Sociology* 78, no 6 (May 1973).

14 S Parker and S Wright, *Inclusion, Innovation and Democracy:
    Growing talent for the creative and cultural industries* (London:
    Demos, 2007).

15 Make Your Mark, *Mind the Gap: From youth enterprise aspirations to
    business creation and growth*, full report, 2007, see
    www.makeyourmark.org.uk/static/uploads/policy/files/
    mind_the_gap.pdf (accessed 14 Jun 2008).

16 See www.kansascityfed.org/publicat/commaffrs/ 07%20Acs.pdf
    (accessed 14 Jun 2008).

17 See for example Open Coffee Club at www.opencoffeeclub.org/
    (accessed 14 Jun 2008).

18 Make Your Mark, *Mind the Gap*.

19 Authors' analysis is based on data from the *Fourth European
    Working Conditions Survey (2005)*, see www.eurofound.europa.eu/
    ewco/surveys/EWCS2005/index.htm (accessed 17 Jun 2008).

20 A Atherton, 'Mapping enterprise: challenges and constraints in
    developing spatial measures and indicators of entrepreneurial
    activity', paper presented at the RGS-IBS Annual Conference,
    London, 2007.

9 To be your own boss: enterprise and emancipation

Tim Campbell and Shawnee B Keck

You don't have anything if you don't have respect.
Charlie, 17

No one is allowed to shout at me, I don't care whose boss they are.
Tom, 16

I like working at the market because I can work my own schedule, the bosses are nice, and if I don't show up I can always come back, they aren't like regular employers.
Abby, 17

What do people who are not in employment, education or training do all day? The answer, perhaps surprisingly, is that some of these so-called NEETS[1] are extremely busy. While their friends might be hanging out, others are selling or trading DVDs, drugs, bikes or self-produced CDs. Their activities are not always legal or desirable, but they can be entrepreneurial as they watch for markets, understand product differentiation, vie for larger sums of backing for the next thing, and, internalise risk into their accounting. As one personal adviser from Connexions explained, 'even the leaders of gangs are being enterprising as they turn illegal goods into a way to buy food and pay rent'.

The situation with NEETs in the UK today is worrying. Debates on a 'lost generation' of over 150,000 young people who are 20 times more likely to commit a crime and 22 times more likely to be a teenage mum dominate the media and policy debates. Areas like the borough of Barking and Dagenham, deemed the 'NEET capital' of Britain with a quarter of teenagers out of school and without a job, are targeted with initiatives aimed at providing advice services or training. Yet there is still untapped potential in encouraging enterprising behaviour among NEET young people.

This chapter argues that acknowledging these behaviours from the start and providing the right guidance could help at-risk young people to make the most of their drive for self-employment and focus on more productive activities. Identifying this entrepreneurial talent can catch young people before they fall, and turn them into legitimate businesspeople. However, achieving this goal relies on the recognition of the potential for internal change stemming from the emotional and psychological effects of being one's 'own boss'. Past examples of economically marginalised groups, such as migrants, testify to the power of enterprise in building people's self-confidence. NEET young people constitute another example of a group who may benefit from the empowerment that enterprise potentially offers.

Enterprising tendencies

NEET is a loose category – one that may include teenage mothers, young offenders or care leavers. They all have different needs and experiences and not all may find enterprise appealing. However, the Make Your Mark campaign in Liverpool, the Local Government Association and the Bright Ideas Trust (BIT) have also uncovered a distinct group that might be described as 'drifting opportunists', or 'floating NEETs'. Social, creative, easily bored, and with a love of risk, members of this group have many of the attributes that small businesspeople need. But they can only realise their potential if they get help to overcome their lack of aspiration and self-belief.

Traditional approaches to training and development for these 'drifting opportunists' do not often work. Fifty-five per cent of respondents in a BIT survey said they would rather turn to crime or state benefits than 'work for someone else'.[2] The third most popular answer to the survey was their desire to continue trying to get their business started, while what the respondents were unlikely to do next seemed to be going back to college to obtain new skills or look for a job.

Like other excluded groups, the ability to control their own lives was mentioned as fundamental for many NEETs in today's Britain. As the quotes at the beginning of this chapter suggest, young people who have consciously rejected institutional forms of learning are hardly likely to want to go into a poorly paid menial job. Being in control of their own working lives and, ideally, their earnings is key to building their confidence and, to some extent, their empowerment.

Since the 1990s, several studies[3] have explored the possibility of enterprise training for some unemployed youth and for particular types of offenders. While the research is made of small samples and pilot projects, the general theory is based on the profile match between the skills it takes to survive on the streets and the perseverance required to run a small business.[4] There is an increasing recognition of the value in encouraging the entrepreneurial behaviours of these groups; it gives a starting point from which to build training programmes; it provides a positive place to start rehabilitation, and is an opportunity for people with few to no qualifications in the formal economy to build skills and competencies.[5] It also builds and cultivates self-esteem.

When considering policy directions for young people at risk, it is essential to understand why they want to strike out on their own. Their motivations are often reduced to a simple case of being rejected by mainstream employers – in other words, the entrepreneur has turned to self-employment for survival. In many interviews we conducted with NEET young people, 'not finding a job they liked' and 'a desire to be independent' were cited as some of the main reasons for their situation. They may not have a big idea, and they may not have an ingenious way to produce something, but they aspire to control their own path and do what they can to keep that control.

The spirit of independence and agency seems to be a core value for this group: 69 per cent stated entrepreneurship was a good career move. For many young people, 'being their own boss' is about being able to make decisions about time, place, content and personal relationships that characterise their working life. It is about agency, or the ability to define 'one's own goals and act upon them'. It is the 'power within', to decide for oneself, it is 'meaning, motivation and purpose', and it is 'the power to... referring to people's capacity to define their own life choices and to pursue their own goals, even in the face of opposition, dissent and resistance from others'.[6]

As many of the viewpoints in this collection also highlight, entrepreneurs most often explain the need for 'power to' as the rationale for starting their own business: 'to be my own boss, to be independent, to challenge myself'. There is a crucial piece of information contained in the mindsets of those who long to control their own economic activity. It is not entrepreneurship for creative innovation and invention; rather, it's about increasing or re-building self-esteem. NEET young people are not the first to articulate the value of this kind of economic agency. In Britain, social and economic marginalisation affects many groups in society, with disproportionate effects for women, migrants, certain ethnic minorities, young people, the unemployed, and intersections of each of these categories. These groups are by no means homogenous and the multiplicity of their needs and experiences is not to be assumed away.

However, evidence shows that whether because of historical job segregation, socially constructed inflexibilities in work arrangements, or a lack of past investment, these people do not fit into the wage labour system in a way that best maximises their earnings and talents. As a result, they often wish to or decide to exit wage work, or more importantly want to. Understanding and listening to their experiences enables us to draw out lessons about how enterprise has benefited them.

For example, African immigrants in the UK comment on their push towards enterprise in interviews with Professor Sonny Sonny Nwankwo from the University of East London Business School:[7]

I felt I could do better than the raw deal I was getting... The crunch came when an individual who, very much my junior, was given a post that literally made him my boss.
Financial adviser

*I am not exactly sure what it was, but you felt treated like an outsider... you
are in no doubt that you don't belong... I thought I was beginning to waste
my time. I could do a lot more on my own, for myself... you do all the hard
stuff but get little of the glory.*
Auditor

Women entrepreneurs tell similar stories. In the US, some
studies show how women mentioned 'the glass ceiling' as their
primary reason for leaving their careers and becoming
entrepreneurs. Information about their experience in wage work
hints at what they are looking for in going into business for
themselves:[8]

· 47 per cent said their contributions were not recognised
  or valued
· 34 per cent said they were not taken seriously
· 29 per cent report feeling isolated as one of few minorities
· 27 per cent saw others being promoted ahead of them

This is not to say that everyone experiences discrimination
in the same way; however, this evidence shows some
commonalities between the two groups. They both list being
passed up for promotion and not feeling valued as primary
factors pushing them into self-employment. Previous Demos
research reveals how 'floating or drifting' NEET young people
have had similar experiences.[9] In particular, the research
uncovered that young people in many areas around the country
do develop their economic agency through enterprise as a means
of overcoming harmful experiences and regaining confidence,
but not always in the formal economy.

It is important to be realistic about the potential of
enterprise in transforming young people's lives. Even those who
do start successful businesses are likely to find themselves
clustered in small return sectors such as business and
manufacturing. They are also likely to suffer from the same
barriers that other marginalised entrepreneurs suffer – including
the difficulty in accessing finance or less developed social
networks and an emphasis on businesses that are 'culturally

appropriate'. Even successful small businesses often have to scrape by.

So why do they do it? What does it mean to control your own economic agency and what can we learn from those who seek it? Microcredit and microenterprise literature from the UK and developing countries provides a solid case study of the question of whether or not economic agency facilitates self-esteem in individuals. The local independence that micro-entrepreneurs say they experience often changes their outlook: economic agency tends to have a positive impact on their wellbeing, even if they are still struggling financially.[10] These testimonies lend support to the idea that enterprise has an emotional element, it's not just about building a business, but also about building up the spirit of the business owner. Entrepreneurship, then, is more about the quality of experience in working life, a focus on exploration, creativity and personal achievement.[11] Citizens are often more likely to be involved in an economy that they feel they help to create through their daily work.

The power of enterprise to empower works at both ends of the spectrum. Even after winning *The Apprentice*, and working for Sir Alan Sugar at Amstrad, one of the authors of this chapter still desperately wanted to become his own boss. Tim left Sugar's business because he felt his task was complete and he wanted to do something independently – the apprenticeship was finished. His goal was to learn some of the business world's secrets and put them into action for his own endeavours, in his own social enterprise and private business.

Unleashing enterprise

Research by BIT, surveying aspiring, but currently unemployed, business owners between the ages of 16 and 30 in Glasgow, Manchester, Birmingham and London shows that, despite the fact that young people stated their desire to own a business, they experienced frustration and confusion on how to get there.[12] In the course of our research, we met 16-year-olds who have had their enterprise training and have come out buzzing to create a business. They have finally found something they can get excited about, but they don't know where to go or who to turn to.

Small efforts on the part of business and policy could yield larger pay-offs in this area. When asked why their businesses failed, 82 per cent of 16–30-year-olds said: 'because I did not know who to turn to' when faced with adversity in start-up; when asked if they knew how to write a business plan, 74 per cent of 16–21-year-olds and 57 per cent of 22–30-year-olds said no; 82 per cent of those surveyed reported that their business did not get past the first stage of development, while 77 per cent of them reported needing £5,000 or less to get started. These figures may demonstrate a powerful intention but even more, the wearisome reality.

Expanding the benefits of enterprise to new people is a job for everyone. It is the responsibility of government to provide a level, equal, social context and to run world-class schools or decent training programmes where skills can be developed and nurtured. If the right policy infrastructure is not in place, and accessible support services remain unavailable, the 'marginal worker will become the marginal entrepreneur' and we are likely to witness a repeat of the same social exclusion and discrimination scenarios that force groups who experience disadvantage to leave employed work in the first place.[13]

However, it is not the job of government to mentor budding entrepreneurs or help them write a good business plan. Young people who are drifting NEETs explain how government help can go only so far, and encouraging entrepreneurship is also a job for the private sector. When BIT asked the question, 'when you began to look at ways of financing your business who did you turn to for help?', 38 per cent said business angels or venture capitalists, and 28 per cent said friends or family. Only 7 per cent said banks and 10 per cent said government, the rest responded charitable trusts. If young entrepreneurs need start-up capital, social networks and mentors, government is not the place to go. The future face of enterprise increasingly entails a partnership between business and government, each with its own strengths.

In order to reinforce this partnership, business leaders (especially at the local level) can transform their company's role in society by giving time, money and advice to foster the economic agency that is often already strong within these groups. One of the best places to learn about business development is to intern or work as an apprentice within one. Established business people are the most potent tool in reaching out to potential entrepreneurs.

The focus on economically excluded groups in local authorities, in education and in the government's employment strategies is growing. When it comes to NEET young people, some suggest that not having anything to do is what drives things like gun crime, or anti-social behaviour. However, it becomes clear how, for some of these people, there is a personal drive for independence that can be turned around. Only when government and business fully understand the possible public benefits of the emotional aspects of enterprise, and how to best tap into this potential, can society truly utilise this energy for positive results.

Tim Campbell is founder of the Bright Ideas Trust and an entrepreneur. Shawnee Keck is a regeneration consultant for the Economics and Development team at URS Corporation Ltd.

Viewpoint
Derek Browne, founder and chief executive of Entrepreneurs in Action (EIA)

Since leaving an inner-city state school, I combined a career as an international athlete and investment banker before becoming a social entrepreneur. Since then, I have dedicated my life to improving young people's understanding and appreciation of the need for employability and entrepreneurship.

Britain has a modern enterprise economy. It is fast moving, increasingly international and service based. The days of large, monolithic top-down command and control by employers are over. Today's economy needs people who understand how businesses and organisations work and are excited by the idea of helping to grow or even starting a business or enterprise.

The problem is that our education system is based on the old style command and control economy. Today's schools have much more in common with the schools of the 1950s and 1960s than businesses do with their counterparts from the same period. So what needs to change?

First of all, it is vital that teaching of soft business skills like problem solving, team work and communication become a core part of the curriculum and not once a year, one week add-ons. There needs to be an increase in business specialists delivering more enterprise education programmes. Business's part in helping to create an enterprising culture is to seriously engage with schools and colleges offering extensive and worthwhile work experience.

Second, school performance should be measured not just on exam results but also on their ability to guide young people into jobs. At the moment there are schools that claim their specialisation is business but that cannot demonstrate the value they add to the economy in any measurable form. For example how many of their students set up businesses after they leave school? Action here would lead to a better return on taxpayers' investment in education.

Finally, it is crucial that every subject taught should have a careers and business angle. Young people need to understand what the value is of what they are learning beyond the classroom and how it will help them in the future. For example, science is not just useful for those who want a career based in science but is also vital in teaching the research and analytical skills that anyone working in today's modern knowledge-based service economy needs.

Too many young people today are rejecting school as not relevant to their lives. The effective integration of employability and entrepreneurial skills into our schools would go a long way to re-engage some of these disaffected pupils.

Notes

1   People who are not in education, employment or training.

2   T Campbell, *Perceptions and Intentions: Entrepreneurship in four cities in the UK* (London: Bright Ideas Trust, 2007).

3   RW Fairlie, 'Drug dealing and legitimate self-employment', *Journal of Labor Economics* 20, no 3 (2002); A Rieple, 'Offenders and entrepreneurship', *European Journal on Criminal Policy and Research* 6, no 2 (1998); P Bourgois, *In Search of Respect: Selling crack in El Barrio* (Cambridge and New York: Cambridge University Press, 1996).

4   H Metcalf, T Anderson and H Rolte, *Barriers to Employment for Offenders and Ex-offenders*, Department for Work and Pensions, research report 155 (London: Centre for Economic and Social Inclusion, 2002).

5   The Prince's Trust, *Reaching the Hardest to Reach* (London: Prince's Trust, 2004).

6   N Kabeer, 'The conditions and consequences of choice: reflections on the measurement of women's empowerment', United Nations Research Institute for Social Development (UNRISD), discussion paper 108 (1999).

7   S Nwankwo, 'Characterisation of Black African entrepreneurship in the UK: a pilot study', *Journal of Small Business and Enterprise Development* 12, no 1 (2005).

8   M Mattis, '"I'm out of here": women leaving companies in the USA to start their own businesses' in S Fielden and M Davidson (eds), *International Handbook of Women and Small Business Entrepreneurship* (Cheltenham, UK: Edward Elgar, 2005); H Green and S Parker, *The Other Glass Ceiling* (London: Demos, 2006).

9   S Keck and T Richardson, *A Case Study of NEETs in Knowsley: A report for Connexions* (London: Demos, 2007).

10 A Bernasek, 'Banking on social change: Grameen Bank lending to women', *International Journal of Politics, Culture, and Society* 16, no 3 (Spring 2003); StreetCred, *Making Microcredit Work: An East London journey* (London: StreetCred, 2007).

11 B Bjerke, *Understanding Entrepreneurship* (Cheltenham, UK, and Northampton, MA: Edward Elgar, 2007).

12 Campbell, *Perceptions and Intentions*.

13 K Mirchandani, 'Women's entrepreneurship: exploring new avenues' in Fielden and Davidson (eds), *International Handbook of Women and Small Business Entrepreneurship*.

10 The five minds for the future

Howard Gardner

At the start of the third millennium, we are well attuned to considerations of 'the future'. In conceptualising the future, I refer to trends whose existence is widely acknowledged: the increasing power of science and technology, the interconnectedness of the world in economic, cultural and social terms, and the incessant circulation and intermingling of human beings of diverse backgrounds and aspirations.

As someone who has witnessed discussions of the future all over the world, I can attest that belief in the power of education – for good or for ill – is ubiquitous. We have little difficulty in seeing education as an enterprise – indeed, the enterprise – for shaping the mind of the future.

What kind of minds should we be cultivating for the future? Five types stand out to me as being particularly urgent at the present time. One by one, let me bring them onto centre stage. And in each case, I'll demonstrate the relation of this mind to entrepreneurship.

The disciplined mind

In English, the word 'discipline' has two distinct connotations. First, we speak of the mind as having mastered one or more disciplines – arts, crafts, professions, scholarly pursuits. By rough estimates, it takes approximately a decade for an individual to learn a discipline well enough so that he or she can be considered an expert or master. Perhaps at one time, an individual could rest on her laurels once such disciplinary mastery has been initially achieved. No longer! Disciplines themselves change, ambient conditions change, as do the demands on individuals who have achieved initial mastery. One must continue to educate oneself and others over succeeding decades.

Such hewing of expertise can be done only if an individual possesses discipline – in the second sense of the word. That is, one needs continually to practise in a disciplined way if one is to remain at the top of one's game.

We first acquire a 'disciplined mind' in school, though relatively few of us go on to become academic disciplinarians. The rest of us master disciplines that are not, strictly speaking, 'scholarly'; yet the need to master a 'way of thinking' applies to the entire range of workers – whether it be lawyers, engineers, crafts persons, or business professionals involved in personnel, marketing, sales or management. Such education may take place in formal classes or on the job, explicitly or implicitly. In the end, a form of mastery will be achieved, one that must continue to be refined over the years.

Nowadays, the mastery of more than one discipline is at a premium. Scholars and universities are increasingly recognising the relationship between interdisciplinary experience and entrepreneurship and it is in this realm that the space is created for truly disruptive business ideas. We value those who are interdisciplinary, multidisciplinary or transdisciplinary. But these claims must be cashed in. The reason we value bilingual people is that they speak more than one language. By the same token, the claim of pluri-disciplinarity (if you'll excuse the neologism) only makes sense if a person has genuinely mastered more than one discipline and can integrate them. For most of us, the attainment of multiple perspectives is a more reasonable goal.

An entrepreneur requires both senses of discipline. She must be able to focus sharply on a goal and work steadily to achieve it. And she must either acquire the disciplines relevant to the realm of the particular entrepreneur or be able to attract experts with the desired discipline.

The synthesising mind

Nobel Laureate in Physics Murray Gell-Mann, an avowed multidisciplinarian, has made an intriguing claim about our times. He asserts that, in the twenty-first century, the most valued mind will be the synthesising mind: the mind that can survey a wide range of sources, decide what is important and worth paying attention to, and then put this information together in ways that make sense to oneself and, ultimately, to others as well.

Gell-Mann is on to something important. Information has never been in short supply. But with the advent of new technologies and media, most notably the internet, vast, seemingly indigestible amounts of information now deluge us around the clock. Shrewd triage becomes an imperative. Those who can synthesise well for themselves will rise to the top of their pack; and those whose syntheses make sense to others will be invaluable teachers, communicators and leaders.

Let's take an example from business. Suppose that you are an executive and your firm is considering the acquisition of a new company in an area that seems important, but about which you and your immediate associates know little. Your goal is to acquire enough information so that you and your board can make a judicious decision, and you need to do so in the next two months. The place to begin is with any existing synthesis: fetch it, devour it and evaluate it. If none exists, you turn to the most knowledgeable individuals and ask them to provide the basic information requisite to synthesis. Given this initial input, you then decide what information seems adequate and where important additional data are required.

At the same time, you need to decide on the form and format of the ultimate synthesis: a written narrative, an oral presentation, a set of scenarios, a set of charts and graphs, perhaps a discussion of pros and cons leading to a final judgement. At last, the actual work of synthesis begins in earnest. New information must be acquired, probed, evaluated, followed up or sidelined. The new information needs to be fitted, if possible, into the initial synthesis; and where fit is lacking, mutual adjustments must be made. Constant reflection is the order of the day.

At some point before the final synthesis is due, a proto-synthesis should be developed. This interim version needs to be tested with the most knowledgeable audience of associates, preferably an audience that is critical and constructive. To the extent that time and resources are available, more than one trial run is desirable. But ultimately there arrives a moment of truth, at which point the best possible synthesis must suffice.

What kind of mind is needed to guide the synthesis? Clearly, though he should have a home area of expertise, the synthesiser cannot conceivably be an expert of every relevant discipline. As compensation, the synthesiser must know enough about the requisite disciplines to be able to make judgements about whom and what to trust – or to identify individuals who can help make that determination. The synthesiser must also have a sense of the relevant forms and formats for the synthesis, being prepared to alter when possible, or advisable, but to make a final commitment as the deadline approaches.

The synthesiser, and especially one involved in launching new enterprises, must always keep her eyes on the big picture, while making sure that adequate details are secured and arranged in useful ways. This is a tall order, but it is quite possible that certain individuals are blessed with a 'searchlight intelligence' – the capacity to look widely and to monitor constantly, thus making sure that nothing vital is missing; and that they also have the capacity to value the complementary 'laser intelligence' that has fully mastered a specific discipline. Such individuals should be identified and cherished.

It is crucial that we determine how to nurture synthesising capacities more widely through and outside of education, since they are likely to remain at a premium in the coming era. This is a mind set recognised in leadership training but often not given enough attention in entrepreneurship education. The emerging potential of web 2.0 technologies only emphasises the premium on those 'synthesisers' to scan the vast amount of information available to spot the genuine entrepreneurial opportunities.

The creating mind

In our time, nearly every practice that is well understood will be automated. Mastery of existing disciplines will be necessary, but not sufficient. The creating mind forges new ground. In our society we have come to value those individuals who keep casting about for new ideas and practices, monitoring their successes, and so on. And we give special honour to those rare individuals whose innovations actually change the practices of their peers – in my trade, we call these individuals 'Big C' creators.

As a student of creativity, I had long assumed that creating was primarily a cognitive feat – having the requisite knowledge and the apposite cognitive processes. But I have come to believe that personality and temperament are equally and perhaps even more important for the would-be creator. More than willing, the creator must be eager to take chances, to venture into the unknown, to fall flat on her face, and then, smiling, pick herself up and once more throw herself into the fray. This is why attention to the appropriate positive attitudes is so important for entrepreneurship education and must not be ignored. Even when successful, the creator does not rest on her laurels. She is motivated again to venture into the unknown and to risk failure, buoyed by the hope that another breakthrough may be in the offing.

This mindset will be familiar – certainly venture capitalists have their sights firmly trained on these people. Indeed, the creator is a close cousin to the entrepreneur, though the former may be more excited by the intellectual breakthrough while the latter's satisfaction comes from launching a new organisation and seeing it grow.

It is important to ascertain the relation among the three kinds of minds introduced thus far. Clearly, synthesising is not possible without some mastery of constituent disciplines – and perhaps there is, or will be, a discipline of synthesising, quite apart from such established disciplines as mathematics, mime or management. I would suggest that creation is unlikely to emerge in the absence of some disciplinary mastery, and, perhaps, some capacity to synthesise as well.

The respectful mind

Almost from the start, infants are alert to other human beings. The attachment link between parent (typically mother) and child is predisposed to develop throughout the early months of life;

and the nature and strength of that bond in turn determines much about the capacity of individuals to form relationships with others throughout life.

Of equal potency is the young human's capacity to distinguish among individuals, and among groups of individuals. We are wired to make such distinctions readily; indeed our survival depends on our ability to distinguish among those who would help and nourish us, and those who might do us harm. But the messages in our particular environment determine how we will label particular individuals or groups. Our own experiences, and the attitudes displayed by the peers and elders to whom we are closest, determine whether we like, admire or respect certain individuals and groups; or whether, on the contrary, we come to shun, fear or even hate these individuals.

We live in an era when nearly every individual is likely to encounter thousands of individuals personally, and when billions of people have the option of travelling abroad or of encountering individuals from remote cultures through visual or digital media. A person possessed of a respectful mind welcomes this exposure to diverse persons and groups. A truly cosmopolitan individual gives others the benefit of the doubt; displays initial trust; tries to form links; avoids prejudicial judgements.

The threats to respect are intolerance and prejudice, what in the worst case forms into individual, state or stateless terrorism. A prejudiced person has preconceived ideas about individuals and groups, and resists bracketing those preconceptions. An intolerant person has a very low threshold for unfamiliarity; the default assumption is that 'strange is bad'. It is not easy to come to respect others whom you have feared, distrusted or disliked. Yet, in an interconnected world, such a potential for growth, for freshly forged or freshly renewed respect, is crucial.

The value of networks and networking as an integral part of entrepreneurial success is widely acknowledged. However, within this, the entrepreneur can only benefit from having an open and respectful mind that values diverse backgrounds and viewpoints. Otherwise, she needlessly handicaps herself in building up an enterprise and managing future relationships.

The ethical mind

An ethical stance is in no way antithetical to a respectful one, but it involves a much more sophisticated stance towards individuals and groups. A person possessed of an ethical mind is able to think of himself abstractly: he is able to ask, 'What kind of a person do I want to be? What kind of a worker do I want to be? What kind of a citizen do I want to be?'

Going beyond the posing of such questions, the person is able to think about herself in a universalistic manner: 'What would the world be like, if all persons behaved the way that I do, if all workers in my profession took the stance that I have, if all citizens in my region or my world carried out their roles in the way that I do?' Such conceptualisation involves a recognition of rights and responsibilities attendant to each role. And crucially, the ethical individual behaves in accordance with the answers that she has forged, even when such behaviours clash with her own self-interest.

My own insights into the ethical mind come from a dozen years of study of professionals who are seeking to do good work – work that is excellent, engaging and ethical (see www.goodworkproject.org). Determining what is ethical is not always easy, and can prove especially challenging during times, like our own, when conditions are changing very quickly, and when market forces are powerful and unmitigated. Even when one has determined the proper course, it is not always easy to behave in an ethical manner; and that is particularly so when one is highly ambitious, when others appear to be cutting corners, when different interest groups demand contradictory things from workers, when the ethical course is less clear than one might like, and when such a course runs against one's immediate self-interest.

It is so much easier, so much more natural, to develop an ethical mind when one inhabits an ethical environment. But such an environment is neither necessary nor sufficient. Crucial contributions are made by the atmosphere at one's first places of work: how do the adults in power behave, what are the beliefs and behaviours of one's peers, and, perhaps above all, what happens when there are clear ethical deviations, and – more happily if less frequently – when an individual or a group behaves in an ethically exemplary fashion? Education in ethics may not begin as early as education for respect; but neither 'curriculum' ever ends.

Of course, entrepreneurs should be ethical and the ethics of business must receive constant attention. And in the long run, those who are ethical will emerge as successful. But faced with new opportunities in an unfamiliar environment, entrepreneurs are often tempted to cut corners, or to pretend to be ignorant of laws or norms. Thus entrepreneurs need special vigilance in the ethical realm.

Given the high standards necessary for an ethical mind, examples of failures abound. It is not difficult to recognise behaviours that are strictly illegal – like theft or fraud – or behaviours that are obviously unethical – the journalist who publishes a story that he knows is not true, the geneticist who overlooks data that run counter to her hypothesis. In each case, the ethical mind must go through the exercise of identifying the kind of individual one wants to be. And when one's own words and behaviours run counter to that idealisation, one must take corrective action. I would add that as one gets older, it does not suffice simply to keep one's own ethical house in order. One acquires a responsibility over the broader realm of which one is a member. And so, for example, an individual journalist or geneticist may behave in an ethical manner, but if her peers are failing to do so, the aging worker should assume responsibility for the health of the domain. I denote such individuals as 'trustees': veterans who are widely respected, deemed to be disinterested, and dedicated to the health of the domain. To quote the French playwright Molière: 'We are responsible not only for what we do but for what we don't do.'[1]

Tensions between and among these minds

Of the five minds, the ones most likely to be confused with one another are the respectful mind and the ethical mind. In part, this is because of ordinary language: we consider respect and ethics to be virtues, and we assume that one cannot have one without the other. Moreover, very often they are correlated; persons who are ethical are also respectful, and vice versa.

However, as indicated, I see these as developmentally discrete accomplishments. One can be respectful from early childhood, even without having a deep understanding of the reasons for respect. In contrast, ethical conceptions and behaviours presuppose an abstract, self-conscious attitude: a capacity to step away from the details of daily life and to think of oneself as a worker, a builder or as a citizen.

Whistle blowers are a good example. Many individuals observe wrongdoing at high levels in their company and remain silent. They may want to keep their jobs, but they also want to respect their leaders. It takes both courage and a mental leap to think of oneself not as an acquaintance of one's supervisor, but rather as a member of an institution or profession, with certain obligations attendant thereto. The whistle blower assumes an ethical stance, at the cost of a respectful relation to his supervisor.

Sometimes, respect may trump ethics. Initially, I believed that the French government was correct in banning Muslim women from wearing scarves at school. By the same token, I defended the right of Danish newspapers to publish cartoons that poked fun at Islamic fundamentalism. In both cases, I was taking the American Bill of Rights at face value – no state religion, guaranteed freedom of expression. But I eventually came to the conclusion that this ethical stance needed to be weighed against the costs of disrespecting the sincere and strongly held religious beliefs of others. The costs of honouring the Islamic preferences seem less than those of honouring an abstract principle. Of course, I make no claim that I did the right thing – only that the tension between respect and ethics can be resolved in contrasting ways.

There is no strict hierarchy among the minds, such that one should be cultivated before the others. Yet a certain rhythm does exist. One needs a certain amount of discipline – in both senses of the term – before one can undertake a reasonable synthesis; and if the synthesis involves more than one discipline, then each of the constituent disciplines needs to be cultivated. By the same token, any genuinely creative activity presupposes a certain discipline mastery. And while prowess at synthesising may be unnecessary, nearly all creative breakthroughs – whether in the arts, politics, scholarship or corporate life – are to some extent dependent on provisional syntheses. Still, too much discipline clashes with creativity; and those who excel at syntheses are less likely to effect the most radical creative breakthroughs.

In the end it is desirable for each person to have achieved aspects of all five minds for the future. Such a personal integration is most likely to occur if individuals are raised in environments where all five kinds of minds are exhibited and valued. So much the better, if there are role models – parents, teachers, masters, supervisors – who display aspects of discipline, synthesis, creation, respect and ethics on a regular basis. In addition to embodying these kinds of minds, the best educators at school or work can provide support, advice and coaching which will help to inculcate discipline, encourage synthesis, prod creativity, foster respect and encourage an ethical stance.

No one can compel the cultivation and integration of the five minds. The individual human being must come to believe that the minds are important, merit the investment of significant amounts of time and resources, and are worthy of continuing nurturance, even when external supports have faded. The individual must reflect on the role of each of these minds at work, in a favoured avocation, in starting a business, at home, in the community and in the wider world. The individual must be aware that sometimes these minds will find themselves in tension with one another, and that any resolution will be purchased at some cost. In the future, the form of mind that is likely to be at greatest premium, to entrepreneurship and more widely, is the synthesising mind. And so it is perhaps fitting that the melding of the minds within an individual's skin is the ultimate challenge of personal synthesis.

Howard Gardner is the Hobbs Professor of Cognition and Education at the Harvard Graduate School of Education. He is the author of many books on psychology, education and policy.

Viewpoint
Linda Austin, headteacher, Swanlea School, Business and Enterprise College

In inner-city schools like ours, enterprise education changes lives. It creates optimism and embeds a culture of success right across the school. This is incredibly important in our area, which is one of the most deprived in the country and where unemployment is six times the national average.

We are developing a world-class enterprise and entrepreneurship programme. Our approach engages and re-engages learners by helping them see connections between the subjects they are learning in real situations. Our teachers incorporate enterprise into everything they do. They not only teach enterprise subjects, they themselves demonstrate what it means to be enterprising to the students. They provide constant examples of the thinking patterns, communication styles and behaviours that we want our students to learn and adopt.

Developing outstanding partnerships with business is also very important for us. We are an enterprising school, but we also recognise that we need partnerships and pathways to give our students the breadth of experiences they need. We think that the relationship we have developed with Merrill Lynch through the Merrill Lynch Enterprise and Entrepreneurship Programme has set a new standard for how schools and businesses can work together.

We are teaching our students to be enterprising in their whole approach to learning and work so they are prepared for the challenges they will face when they become adults. The future is uncertain. It is notoriously difficult to predict future markets or what skills businesses will need. So we feel it is incredibly important for our students to have the ability to learn about new things and tackle new problems as situations require. Whatever path they choose, our school is striving to make sure that our students are well equipped to make the future bright.

Notes

1 Original: 'Nous sommes responsables non seulement de ce que nous faisons, mais aussi de ce que nous ne faisons pas', Molière (Jean-Baptiste Poquelin).

Afterword

Peter Grigg and Alessandra Buonfino

This collection of essays has highlighted some of the perspectives that will increasingly define the shape of enterprise in the UK. We have brought together voices from the frontline of this cultural revolution and uncovered a 'long tail' of change that stretches and winds its way through basements and small offices, the web and corporations. This final chapter attempts to summarise the key themes that provide fertile territory for policy consideration and challenges that could be addressed to support the future success of potential entrepreneurs.

The chapters and viewpoints in this collection hint at a conclusion that, in many ways, resonates with that found in the 2008 Enterprise Strategy:[1] the UK today already has a more enterprising culture but much remains to be done. This collection has demonstrated that change is happening in different places, in different ways and in different sectors. It has highlighted that globalisation is not an event but a journey that requires constant evaluation along the way about the best next steps. At least six major challenges stand out that remain for the future success of UK enterprise and overcoming them will be the key to creating an enterprise culture that is fit for the twenty-first century:

1　There is an urgent need to get to grips with environmental and social change – through new partnerships between business and social entrepreneurs.

2　In a complex and interconnected world, the lone entrepreneur may be a thing of the past. The focus of enterprise support should be on connecting individuals to broader knowledge, networks and experience.

3 Enterprising people will be at the heart of future global competitiveness yet enterprise is missing from debates around 'employability'.

4 Entrepreneurial mindsets are not static but shift over time. Enterprise education should focus on preparing bold, inquisitive, enterprising minds for the future.

5 The UK still needs to challenge stereotypes about who could be tomorrow's entrepreneur. Appealing to new groups of untapped enterprise potential should be based on individual aspirations and passions, not just demographics.

6 A national culture of enterprise will not work unless localities and communities shape enterprising places.

There is an urgent need to get to grips with environmental and social change – through new partnerships between business and social entrepreneurs

One of the major issues that this collection highlights is that budding environmentalists and social entrepreneurs are full of new ideas to address fundamental environmental and social challenges. But as John Elkington points out in chapter 4, the challenge is getting these ideas scaled-up to achieve maximum impact. Too often, a simplistic translation of this challenge hears calls for scaling-up the *size* of successful social enterprises – which in turn can lead to demands that compromise social and environmental missions. For maximum impact, the focus should be on scaling-up the successful *ideas* that can change society and examining the role that big businesses can play in supporting and scaling up the *impact* of these.

According to Vinod Khosla, one of the co-founders of Sun Microsystems, risk and acceptance of failure are central to developing and sharing innovation, but large companies typically avoid both. Smaller enterprises and entrepreneurs might have the answers. As Khosla argues: 'Big companies didn't invent the internet or Google, and much of the big change in telecoms also came from outsiders.'[2] This, it could be argued, is equally true for large public sector employers addressing social needs. So when it comes to addressing the big challenges of society such as climate change or poverty, it may be the disruptive behaviours of social and environmental entrepreneurs, rather than governmental interventions alone, that will make the real breakthrough.

Audretsch, in chapter 1, describes the concept of 'entrepreneurial spill-over' and opens up what has been described by Simon Parker as a 'black box' and a 'highly ambitious research agenda'.[3] What Parker means by this is that while the positive spill-over of entrepreneurial activity is easy to understand when it leads to new inventions or companies, the potential positive impact of entrepreneurship on issues such as improving the environment or reducing societal problems are hugely complex and under-researched areas. The challenge then is to understand how entrepreneurial spill-over can be capitalised on in a way that drives more social entrepreneurship. Commonly, the debate has concentrated on sharing scientific or engineering expertise, but there is as much need to concentrate on how large companies can diffuse other forms of knowledge – such as staff experience and access to networks – in order to play a part in addressing social and environmental concerns.

The future face of enterprise requires both sides to step up and connect through innovative partnerships. For instance, this country has a strong and growing environmental industries sector but increasingly every industry will need to become an environmental industry as consumer demand for responsible businesses and sustainable policies will result in an impact on economic policy. Enterprising responses from businesses could learn from the most innovative solutions emerging from young social entrepreneurs and campaigners. As Grigg and Lacey highlight, young people are increasingly aware of the need for environmental and ethical solutions to business problems and this driver can be used to spur enterprising responses from within big companies.

In a complex and interconnected world, the lone entrepreneur may be a thing of the past. The focus of enterprise support should be on connecting individuals to broader knowledge, networks and experience

Retrospectively, it is possible to say that, historically, enterprise policy might have focused too much on businesses and insufficiently on individuals; and on influencing individual thinking and behaviour. But what is also clear from this collection is that the individual entrepreneurs of tomorrow cannot afford to 'go it alone' without collaboration and support networks. Kulveer Taggar for example describes how the Silicon Valley environment cultivates collaboration and co-operation – people willing to talk, help and network an 'optimistic and ambitious vibe' which rewards big thinking. The world of business has become far more complex and interconnected not least due to the pace of change and specialisation.

Yet, in the face of this, networks and the role of mentors, real or virtual, are widely overlooked in enterprise support despite the fact that they are recognised as a scalable and cost-effective way for potential entrepreneurs to access mentors, financial support and advice from a wide range of actors on the enterprise scene. Too often, young potential and practising entrepreneurs are discouraged from setting up or growing their business by overly formal methods of business support and a lack of local, personalised support for their ideas. The idea of setting up a business often seems daunting and can be affected by a fear of failure and an unwillingness to take the plunge. Networks and mentors in this sense can provide a central part of business support for entrepreneurs.

Technology is a powerful enabler for joining up brainpower in the future world of enterprise – so, for those seeking out like-minded creative friends, risk-takers, experts and potential financiers, it's increasingly vital to seek out new enterprising people and places. YouTube, MySpace, Wikipedia, Bebo, Flickr and so many other sites are other examples of technological advances that are fuelling, and have been fuelled by, the desire for more participation in design and delivery rather than just for passive receipt of entertainment, information or debate. Web 2.0[4] creates so many possibilities for providing advice and support for businesses and educationalists wanting to run effective enterprise-related curricula. Technology can support the desire for personalised, user-generated, on-demand support meaning that top-down, generic approaches to offering business and enterprise support are no longer sufficient. From hints and tips to stories and suggestions, websites such as Enterprise Nation (www.enterprisenation.com), SMARTA (www.smarta.com) and www.startups.co.uk are attempting to pioneer new enterprise spaces. Although we should be wary of thinking of web 2.0 as a panacea, there are clear opportunities to apply this learning in relation to business creation and growth as well as to more creative spaces for education in the era of globalisation.

Enterprising people will be at the heart of future global competitiveness yet enterprise is missing from debates around 'employability'

Gordon Frazer's essay demonstrates that major corporations such as Microsoft value enterprise and innovation as core skills. Even large companies will have to continually reinvent themselves, faced with new styles of flexible, adaptive businesses. Frazer, UK Managing Director of Microsoft, states that 'UK plc is faced with a new business reality. Businesses must encourage the people within their organisations to be more entrepreneurial, if they are to deliver greater levels of meaningful innovation. "Intrapreneurs", those people using their entrepreneurial skills for the benefit of the organisation they work for, are therefore key components in fostering an innovative environment and helping an organisation grow.'[5]

Yet, O'Leary and Skidmore's chapter leads us to ask: to what extent can we be confident that enterprise is regarded as central to the notion of what employers consider as key 'employability' skills? Common debate centres around the skills of literacy, numeracy and communication – all of which are valuable and potentially life-changing skills. Yet, these may not necessarily be the skills that will equip our nation to be enterprising go-getters in the global economy. The Leitch review made clear the huge challenge of the skills deficit in the UK: without increased skills, we will 'condemn ourselves to a lingering decline in competitiveness, diminishing economic growth and a bleaker future for all'.[6] But, in defining this skills deficit in terms of current qualifications, Leitch may have overlooked the point that future economies and communities may well require different skill-sets than those obtained through current qualifications.

The likelihood that young people today are, on average, going to have 19 job changes in their life means that specific qualifications are less relevant than ability to problem-solve, build relationships, apply knowledge and experience, and be able to cope with uncertainty. For example, born in the 1990s this group of children is the first who cannot remember using a computer for the first time. As Demos highlighted in *Their Space*,[7] this younger generation will reinvent workplaces and societies on their terms, along the progressive lines built into the technology they use everyday – networks, collaboration, global interdependence and participation. To prepare for our global futures we need calculated risk-takers, entrepreneurial mindsets, positive attitudes, resourceful, networked leaders. To do this, enterprise needs a place at the heart of concepts of employability so that young people can pick up the skills, attitudes and experiences to make ideas happen.

Entrepreneurial mindsets are not static but shift over time. Enterprise education should focus on preparing bold, inquisitive, enterprising minds for the future

Part of the challenge in creating a more enterprising culture is accepting a broad definition of what it means to be enterprising. Enterprising behaviour today should be sought and encouraged in the campaigner for social or environmental change, as well as in the serial entrepreneur; in the civil servant as much as the business person; the GP as well as the community worker. This will sometimes lead to new business formation, but could equally lead to societal, environmental or workplace innovations. As

Martha Lane Fox suggests, 'creating an enterprise culture in the UK needs to start at home and at school with the encouragement, mentoring, sponsorship and apprenticeship of young people'.

It is encouraging then that awareness of enterprise capability has grown immensely since the injection of funding for schools for activity at Key Stage 4. There is a growing recognition that enterprise education can help raise the aspirations of young people and the proportion of young people participating in enterprise events and activities is rising. Yet, we should not be afraid to ask searching questions about the kinds of mindsets that we will need for the future and how we might integrate these into enterprise education.

Howard Gardner's chapter considers, in the context of a rapidly changing economy, five different mindsets needed in this era. His conceptualisation about ways of thinking and behaving in a global world can help inform our thinking on how the entrepreneurial mind needs to adapt and evolve in the future. Kyle Whitehill of Vodafone believes that the twenty-first century will not be a war between large business and their more agile smaller counterparts, but a war for talent that can be sourced not only in the UK but, increasingly, globally. However we conceptualise the challenge, we should not simply be content to develop enterprise capabilities for today but also contemplate those for tomorrow.

Building the right skills for future enterprise is essential. According to Gardner, the world of the future will demand capacities that, until now, have been mere options. We need to create an agenda that thinks about where next; that examines which programmes and activities, in schools and outside, can cultivate future mindsets. These challenges are not insurmountable – and the best way to overcome them will be to inspire the next generation to use their entrepreneurial energy to drive change. There is already a strong desire among young people to use their ideas for change, but more needs to be done to cultivate the mindsets and foster the support that tomorrow's entrepreneurs will need if young people are not to be discouraged from trying. Having reviewed the level of enterprise within the first diplomas to be taught from next September, Make Your Mark found that enterprise is recognised in most of the first five – the Creative and Media, IT and Engineering diplomas stand out as exemplars.[8] However, there is room for improvement in future diplomas. Those developing the diplomas have a lot on their plates, but the vision for the diplomas should remain one of innovative qualifications that equip learners not just for today's industries, but also with the enterprising capabilities to lead a world we have not yet dreamt of.

The UK still needs to challenge stereotypes about who could be tomorrow's entrepreneur. Appealing to new groups of untapped enterprise potential should be based on individual aspirations and passions, not just demographics

As Iqbal Wahhab, chief executive of The Glorious Group, which owns The Cinnamon Club and Roast, argues in this collection: 'The future face of enterprise has to be different. Society must embrace diversity in enterprise and not pigeon-hole people with stereotyped expectations.' If we are to open up the enterprise playing field, we should encourage the unexpected. Entrepreneurs from groups including women, minorities and the socially excluded can bring new insights and approaches into the business world, and fundamentally challenge negative assumptions about their capabilities. The UK still needs to break down stereotypes – including race and gender – and challenge expectations of entrepreneurship.

In this respect, role models, mentors and inspirational figures can all play a significant role but, in general, why do rates of female start-up in this country remain stubbornly low? And why are there so many ethnic minority groups that, despite being entrepreneurially minded, do not start businesses? Of course there are structural factors at play but could it also be that categorising these groups into traditional 'blocks' is no longer proving sufficiently robust to inspire and support entrepreneurial behaviour? Providing support to unlock the enterprise potential among different groups should be based on entrepreneurial desire and tendencies rather than race, age or gender. As Audretsch highlights, entrepreneurship policy needs to have a greater sensitivity to the environmental conditions that shape the individual decision-making process of entrepreneurs.

New ways are needed to connect to audiences, for example, by breaking down traditional assumptions of entrepreneurship as solely about making money, or by challenging perceptions of entrepreneurship being an overly macho career. Enterprise talent among groups is too often defined in terms of their disadvantage or what they can't do rather than what they can do. The Smallwood report for example highlights the pressing need to support self-employment among the over 50s in a non-patronising way.[9] Enterprise offers an opportunity for individuals to break down stereotypes based on their entrepreneurial talent. This is recognised in the Enterprise Strategy, which sets out a desire for the Make Your Mark campaign to extend its reach to groups beyond young people – such as the over 50s, and women and black and minority ethnic groups of all ages. While enterprise as an 'opportunity for all' policy is not new, the challenge now is to create a narrative that is inclusive but not based on equal opportunities.

To make enterprise a more inclusive sport, society should place a value on those actors who are able to facilitate enterprise activity in a way that has wider benefit. Campbell and Keck's chapter describes one group of young people across the UK where this is certainly worth exploring further; enterprise training was seen to have particular impact for those not in employment, education or training (NEET). The relationship between enterprise and the NEET agenda is still under-explored in the UK, in particular, the essential role of local authorities in doing this. There are opportunities within a range of current policy frameworks to recognise the potential talents of 16–19-year-olds by actively promoting and supporting entrepreneurial activity as one education or training option at this age. The UK has made a good start in building a new and inclusive culture of enterprise, but realising the full potential of this agenda means encouraging the broadest possible range of entrepreneurial activity, and celebrating small wins along the way.

A national culture of enterprise will not work unless localities and communities shape enterprising places

The places of enterprise have changed dramatically in recent years. Buzzing enterprise happens in the most unpredictable places: through the web, across borders, in people's kitchens and living rooms. Jim Lawn's essay highlights some ways through which technology is enabling us to work anywhere and be anywhere – the knowledge economy though is becoming invisible. If you tried to take a snapshot of enterprise in the UK today, you would be likely to miss some of the places where enterprise culture is thriving. For example, 25,000 Britons earned their living solely by trading on eBay at the beginning of 2006. As Peter Day points out, 'the new clusters of enterprise centre on ideas, not coal, steel or cotton, and they are harder to pin on the map'.

Although the relevance of local 'place' is sometimes challenged in this 'flat-world', economic analysis continues to identify local factors, clusters and institutions as major influences on economic change and growth. There are different ways to generate enterprising behaviours locally and so towns and cities across the country have a responsibility to identify, recognise and inspire local enterprise talent. Local government's 'place-shaping' role sees it attempting to use its leadership and influence to 'convene' the economic and social wellbeing of its citizens. This collection makes clear that an enterprise culture should form part of any vibrant place. More needs to be done to build an enterprise culture that fits with local government's place shaping role and to encourage intrapreneurship in all areas.

According to Steve Easterbrook, CEO of McDonald's UK,[10] within this, there is the need to strike the right balance between local and global ambition: '[Coming] from the UK head of a global brand it might sound surprising, but the best examples of enterprise are to be found in local endeavours. Encouraging and enabling local enterprise is good for global business.' According to David Zhang, vice secretary general of the Shanghai Technology Enterpreneurship Foundation for Graduates,[11] start-ups are firmly embedded in a locality – but, increasingly have a global mindset as they strive to compete in an interconnected economy and find new areas of growth: 'At the same time, global players will increasingly have to consider how they respond to the local needs, preferences and culture of customers around the world.' As this collection has highlighted, the lack of economy giants in Europe will have to be redressed by major work in growing the capacity for local, national and regional entrepreneurship. In November 2008, Enterprise Week goes global and over 50 countries around the world so far have signed up to running simultaneous enterprise efforts. By giving young people global experience and understanding the hope is to be able to influence the future international ambition of the companies they develop in the future.

Conclusion

The authors in this collection have painted a picture of a changing world of enterprise – one characterised by new places, new technologies, new skills. For enterprise to really leave its mark, it will need the right terrain for it to thrive on. Building an enterprise culture that is fit for the twenty-first century depends on exploiting these new emerging possibilities. Much will need changing: from what's in our textbooks to how society incentivises risk-taking. This collection of essays has started to conceptualise and articulate some of the key features of the future face of enterprise. Progressing this thinking into ideas for action is now the next challenge.

The future face of enterprise in the UK is an exciting and opportunity-packed place. The ideas and viewpoints emerging from this collection have tried to identify the most potent sources of that energy, understand how it can be harnessed, and encourage, inform and hopefully challenge you to help bring to life a face of enterprise that is fit for the future.

Peter Grigg is principal policy adviser for the Make Your Mark campaign; Alessandra Buonfino is head of research at Demos.

Viewpoint
Gita Patel, director, Stargate Capital Investment Group

Enterprise is the engine of economic growth and as such needs to be seen as a natural choice for people who want to set up businesses – in the same way that people go into professions. I have not come across any entrepreneur who sets up in business to fail – so the questions are: why don't they come out the other side as a successful business and why do we accommodate such high failure rates? For the future of enterprise this needs to be addressed urgently so that we can encourage the entrepreneurial spirit in the UK. This is important because we need a culture that takes calculated risks from an informed base and builds on its success as well as learning from its failure. Resilience and self-belief are paramount and one should not fear failure. We must nurture a culture that does not write you off just because your first idea did not work. This is critical for the future of enterprise because if one business idea does not work, you learn from it and move on to the next idea and bounce back.

We can learn many lessons from immigrant businesses, whether they are lifestyle businesses or high-growth companies. These create value despite facing important barriers in business, including cultural obstacles and lack of access to resources.

One of the most important factors in their success is having an enabling and supportive environment. We need to ensure people have access to capital, to markets and to business networks as well as sharing best practice. Influential capital is hugely important in helping early stage businesses to overcome disadvantages related to size. Collaboration with institutions in the private and public sector also plays a major role by linking entrepreneurs to networks, mentors, supply chains, and so on.

As the word about entrepreneurship spreads, we will see an increase in the number of women and young entrepreneurs, especially where education provides the basic tools for launching an enterprise. Our challenge is to create an environment where those who dare to dream can realise those dreams in business and where we replace stumbling blocks with stepping stones.

Notes

1   HM Treasury, *Enterprise: Unlocking the UK's talent* (London: HM
     Treasury, 2008), available at www.hm-
     treasury.gov.uk/budget/budget_08/documents/bud_bud08_en
     terprise.cfm (accessed 17 Jun 2008).

2   'Something new under the sun', special report, *The Economist*,
     Oct 2007.

3   SC Parker, 'The economics of entrepreneurship: what we know
     and what we don't', *Foundations and Trends in Entreprenurship* 1,
     no 1 (2005).

4   'Web 2.0' refers to a 'second generation' of internet-based
     services that emphasise online collaboration and sharing among
     users, often allowing users to build connections between
     themselves and others. This definition is taken from the Demos
     report *Their Space* where this and among other terms such as
     wikis and blogs are laid out in a useful glossary. See H Green
     and C Hannon, *Their Space: Education for a digital generation*
     (London: Demos, 2007).

5   See www.makeyourmark.org.uk/policy/
     future_face_of_enterprise/who_else/viewpoints/ctoi/
     #ffoegordonfrazer (accessed 17 Jun 2008).

6   Leitch Review of Skills, *Prosperity for All in the Global Economy.
     World class skills*, final report (Norwich: HMSO, 2006), available
     at www.hm-treasury.gov.uk/leitch (accessed 17 Jun 2008).

7   Green and Hannon, *Their Space*.

8   Make Your Mark, 'Articulating enterprise within the 14–19
     diplomas', a Make Your Mark campaign reflection paper, Sep
     2007, available at
     www.makeyourmark.org.uk/static/uploads/policy/files/articulat
     ing_enterprise.pdf (accessed 17 Jun 2008).

9   C Smallwood and L Obiamiwe, *Improving Employment Prospects for the Over 50s* (London: The PRIME Initiative, Jan 2008).

10 Steve Easterbrook's viewpoint for the Future Face of Enterprise is to be found at www.makeyourmark.org.uk/policy/future_face_of_enterprise/who_else/viewpoints/ctoi/#ffoesteveeasterbrook (accessed 17 Jun 2008).

11 David Zhang's viewpoint for the Future Face of Enterprise is to be found at www.makeyourmark.org.uk/policy/future_face_of_enterprise/who_else/viewpoints/stoz/#ffoedavidzhang (accessed 17 Jun 2008).

Demos – Licence to Publish

The work (as defined below) is provided under the terms of this licence ('licence'). The work is protected by copyright and/or other applicable law. Any use of the work other than as authorized under this licence is prohibited. By exercising any rights to the work provided here, you accept and agree to be bound by the terms of this licence. Demos grants you the rights contained here in consideration of your acceptance of such terms and conditions.

1   Definitions

A   **'Collective Work'** means a work, such as a periodical issue, anthology or encyclopedia, in which the Work in its entirety in unmodified form, along with a number of other contributions, constituting separate and independent works in themselves, are assembled into a collective whole. A work that constitutes a Collective Work will not be considered a Derivative Work (as defined below) for the purposes of this Licence.

B   **'Derivative Work'** means a work based upon the Work or upon the Work and other pre-existing works, such as a musical arrangement, dramatization, fictionalization, motion picture version, sound recording, art reproduction, abridgment, condensation, or any other form in which the Work may be recast, transformed, or adapted, except that a work that constitutes a Collective Work or a translation from English into another language will not be considered a Derivative Work for the purpose of this Licence

C   **'Licensor'** means the individual or entity that offers the Work under the terms of this Licence.

D   **'Original Author'** means the individual or entity who created the Work.

E   **'Work'** means the copyrightable work of authorship offered under the terms of this Licence.

F   **'You'** means an individual or entity exercising rights under this Licence who has not previously violated the terms of this Licence with respect to the Work,or who has received express permission from Demos to exercise rights under this Licence despite a previous violation.

2   Fair Use Rights

Nothing in this licence is intended to reduce, limit, or restrict any rights arising from fair use, first sale or other limitations on the exclusive rights of the copyright owner under copyright law or other applicable laws.

3   Licence Grant

Subject to the terms and conditions of this Licence, Licensor hereby grants You a worldwide, royalty-free, non-exclusive,perpetual (for the duration of the applicable copyright) licence to exercise the rights in the Work as stated below:

A   to reproduce the Work, to incorporate the Work into one or more Collective Works, and to reproduce the Work as incorporated in the Collective Works;

B   to distribute copies or phonorecords of, display publicly,perform publicly, and perform publicly by means of a digital audio transmission the Work including as incorporated in Collective Works; The above rights may be exercised in all media and formats whether now known or hereafter devised.The above rights include the right to make such modifications as are technically necessary to exercise the rights in other media and formats. All rights not expressly granted by Licensor are hereby reserved.

4   Restrictions

The licence granted in Section 3 above is expressly made subject to and limited by the following restrictions:

A   You may distribute,publicly display, publicly perform, or publicly digitally perform the Work only under the terms of this Licence, and You must include a copy of, or the Uniform Resource Identifier for, this Licence with every copy or phonorecord of the Work You distribute, publicly display,publicly perform, or publicly digitally perform.You may not offer or impose any terms on the Work that alter or restrict the terms of this Licence or the recipients' exercise of the rights granted hereunder.You may not sublicence the Work.You must keep intact all notices that refer to this Licence and to the disclaimer of warranties.You may not distribute, publicly display, publicly perform, or publicly digitally perform the Work with any technological measures that control access or use of the Work in a manner inconsistent with the terms of this Licence Agreement.The above applies to the Work as incorporated in a Collective Work, but this does not require the Collective Work apart from the Work itself to be made subject to the terms of this Licence. If You create a Collective Work, upon notice from any Licencor You must, to the extent practicable, remove from the Collective Work any reference to such Licensor or the Original Author, as requested.

B   You may not exercise any of the rights granted to You in Section 3 above in any manner that is primarily intended for or directed toward commercial advantage or private monetary compensation.The exchange of the Work for other copyrighted works by means of digital filesharing or otherwise shall not be considered to be intended for or directed toward commercial advantage or private monetary compensation, provided there is no payment of any monetary compensation in connection with the exchange of copyrighted works.

c   If you distribute, publicly display, publicly perform, or publicly digitally perform the Work or any Collective Works,You must keep intact all copyright notices for the Work and give the Original Author credit reasonable to the medium or means You are utilizing by conveying the name (or pseudonym if applicable) of the Original Author if supplied; the title of the Work if supplied. Such credit may be implemented in any reasonable manner; provided, however, that in the case of a Collective Work, at a minimum such credit will appear where any other comparable authorship credit appears and in a manner at least as prominent as such other comparable authorship credit.

5   Representations, Warranties and Disclaimer

A   By offering the Work for public release under this Licence, Licensor represents and warrants that, to the best of Licensor's knowledge after reasonable inquiry:

   i   Licensor has secured all rights in the Work necessary to grant the licence rights hereunder and to permit the lawful exercise of the rights granted hereunder without You having any obligation to pay any royalties, compulsory licence fees, residuals or any other payments;

   ii The Work does not infringe the copyright, trademark, publicity rights, common law rights or any other right of any third party or constitute defamation, invasion of privacy or other tortious injury to any third party.

B   except as expressly stated in this licence or otherwise agreed in writing or required by applicable law,the work is licenced on an 'as is'basis,without warranties of any kind, either express or implied including,without limitation,any warranties regarding the contents or accuracy of the work.

6   Limitation on Liability

Except to the extent required by applicable law, and except for damages arising from liability to a third party resulting from breach of the warranties in section 5, in no event will licensor be liable to you on any legal theory for any special, incidental,consequential, punitive or exemplary damages arising out of this licence or the use of the work, even if licensor has been advised of the possibility of such damages.

7   Termination

A   This Licence and the rights granted hereunder will terminate automatically upon any breach by You of the terms of this Licence. Individuals or entities who have received Collective Works from You under this Licence,however, will not have their licences terminated provided such individuals or entities remain in full compliance with those licences. Sections 1, 2, 5, 6, 7, and 8 will survive any termination of this Licence.

B   Subject to the above terms and conditions, the licence granted here is perpetual (for the duration of the applicable copyright in the Work). Notwithstanding the above, Licensor reserves the right to release the Work under different licence terms or to stop distributing the Work at any time; provided, however that any such election will not serve to withdraw this Licence (or any other licence that has been, or is required to be, granted under the terms of this Licence), and this Licence will continue in full force and effect unless terminated as stated above.

8   Miscellaneous

A   Each time You distribute or publicly digitally perform the Work or a Collective Work, Demos offers to the recipient a licence to the Work on the same terms and conditions as the licence granted to You under this Licence.

B   If any provision of this Licence is invalid or unenforceable under applicable law, it shall not affect the validity or enforceability of the remainder of the terms of this Licence, and without further action by the parties to this agreement, such provision shall be reformed to the minimum extent necessary to make such provision valid and enforceable.

C   No term or provision of this Licence shall be deemed waived and no breach consented to unless such waiver or consent shall be in writing and signed by the party to be charged with such waiver or consent.

D   This Licence constitutes the entire agreement between the parties with respect to the Work licensed here.There are no understandings, agreements or representations with respect to the Work not specified here. Licensor shall not be bound by any additional provisions that may appear in any communication from You.This Licence may not be modified without the mutual written agreement of Demos and You.